BBC

THE GREAT BRITISH YEAR

Wildlife through the Seasons

STEPHEN MOSS

Quercus

IT HAS BEEN SAID that Britain is a nation obsessed with the weather. Historically, the changing weather has been inextricably linked with our survival – good weather ensures a good harvest, while wild weather can mean devastation. So, we humans have learned to work with the changing seasons; our diet is determined by the animals and crops we rear and harvest, just as their survival depends on the lifecycles and seasonal activities of the wider natural world.

The subject of our seasons has long attracted the attention of TV programme-makers, especially those in the world-famous BBC Natural History Unit based in Bristol, but *The Great British Year* uses the latest modern technology to give us the deepest insight yet into our national obsession. Cleverly, the production team challenged the conventional approach of four seasons as distinct from one another, and instead showed how nature actually proceeds in a series of subtle changes that occur from day to day, month to month and season to season.

Thus each of the four programmes in this series covers a three-month period of transition: Winter into Spring, Spring into Summer, Summer into Autumn and finally Autumn into Winter. They do so because what is truly fascinating about the seasons is the way that different plants and animals respond in different ways, and at very different times, to subtle but important changes in day length, temperature and weather.

As we journey from the beginning of the year to its end, we watch the survival secrets of wildlife from across Britain. We begin in midwinter, when dormice, hedgehogs and bats are hibernating in dark corners, conserving vital resources while food is hard to find, while outside plants lie dormant, waiting for the return of the sun and its life-giving rays. Many birds leave our shores for warmer climes, while those who stay behind, like ptarmigans, battle the elements in some of our most extreme landscapes in the Scottish Highlands alongside mountain hares and stoats.

But soon the temperatures rise and the world rouses from its slumber and becomes a scene of great activity. Buds burst, snowdrops and bluebells brighten up our woodlands, animals prepare to breed in extraordinary rituals such as boxing (hares) and lekking (grouse and other birds). Our ponds fill with frogspawn, and if you

are lucky you might catch a glimpse of stag beetles on the wing. As spring rolls into summer Britain is bursting with new life; seal pups prepare for life at sea, butterflies fill the air, glow worms light our way at night and the roadsides are a riot of colour. Animal parents expend great energy in these months of plenty feeding their young, while other animals feed in frenzied preparation for leaner times ahead, feasting on juicy berries in the hedgerows or on the dwindling number of insects, while squirrels stash their secret hoards of nuts and seeds.

Autumn brings the clash of antlers amongst rutting deer, while heroic salmon leap up rivers in their marathon homeward journey. But as the year comes full circle and Britain once more falls quiet in winter, when animals have begun to hibernate and birds have migrated to warmer climes, we can mull over the year that has passed and contemplate the year to come. We also welcome our Arctic visitors as these birds fill the empty skies until spring brings the return of much of our wildlife.

This book will reveal these stories, and more, to paint a picture of Britain and its wildlife throughout the year as a whole, in tandem with the accompanying television series. It will also reveal how this fascinating series was made – despite the challenges faced by the production team during the two-year filming period. And for those of you who reach the end of this story inspired by our British wildlife and eager to see it with your own eyes, there is also a directory of 40 key wildlife events, spectacles and species, and a map showing 20 top places to watch wildlife in Britain throughout the four seasons.

Like many Britons, I love all four of our seasons, and enjoy the buzz of excitement we all feel as each shifts into the next, bringing new natural sights and sounds as it does so. The first swallow of spring and the falling leaves of autumn, the buzz of bumblebees on a hot summer's day and the crunch of snow underfoot in winter are part of what makes us British. So I hope you enjoy what follows: a rollercoaster ride through the four seasons, seen through the eyes of our own, very special wildlife.

STEPHEN MOSS
Somerset, February 2013

WINTER
INTO
SPRING

Winter is the toughest season of all for our wildlife. This truly is a time of life or death: in order to survive these bleak months they must either find food to give them energy, sleep through the winter in a state of hibernation, or head far away from our shores. Birds such as geese and starlings gather in huge flocks, creating amazing spectacles, while mammals such as deer and hares are also very visible – a small compensation for the absence of wild flowers and insect life. But even in this chilly season there are plenty of signs of spring – if you know where to look!

DECEMBER 21 DAWNS much the same as any other winter's day: crisp, clear and cold, or dull, dank and dreary – depending on the prevailing weather conditions. But although the weather may change, from place to place and from year to year, one thing remains constant: sometime between 21 December and the early hours of 22 December, Britain passes through the winter solstice. During this time the sun reaches its lowest point in the sky, and so we experience less daylight than at any other time of year, making it the shortest day.

The worst of winter is yet to come, with all the trials and tribulations that frost, snow and ice will bring for human beings, plants and animals alike. Yet with the solstice there also comes a sense of promise, of rebirth, of new life. For, as with the spring and autumn equinoxes, and the summer solstice, the shortest day is a pivotal moment in our seasons. From now onwards, the Earth begins to tilt back towards the Sun. Gradually, inexorably at first, then faster and faster, the days will lengthen.

Yet the temperature – which other than light is the main influence on life on our planet – continues to fall. Across most of Britain, the coldest temperatures, along with the majority of ice and snow, generally arrive during the months of January and February – even sometimes into March.

Imagine you are a plant or animal, about to face the onset of the toughest period in your life. What options will you have over the next three months, as winter takes its icy hold?

The chances are that you have already made the critical choices that will enable you to survive the winter. Fundamentally, whether you are a bird or butterfly, badger or bumblebee, oak tree or orchid, you will have opted for one of three broad options: sleep, feed or flee.

The key to surviving the winter varies enormously depending on what kind of organism you are, your position in the food chain, and your physiological capacity. For example, birds such as warblers, flycatchers, swallows and swifts have the ability to migrate long distances across the globe to find more amenable places where they can spend the winter months. Indeed, they need to do so, for the small insects on which they feed virtually disappear at this time of year. However, terrestrial mammals such as badgers, foxes, voles and shrews do not have the option to migrate,

so they must stay put for the winter and face the arduous task of finding enough food to enable them to survive these harsh months.

Although bumblebees can, of course, fly, they are unable to cross large areas of water so they cannot migrate; whereas some species of butterflies can migrate but most find other strategies to survive, such as overwintering as adults, eggs or pupae. Plants have no option but to stay put; but even so, different species pursue very different winter-survival strategies from one another.

Some creatures, such as the hedgehog, the dormouse and various species of bat, choose to hibernate, shutting down their systems for the whole of the winter season. For those wildlife that do not either migrate or hibernate there is only one option: during every waking hour they must take advantage of precious daylight to feed. Life is really quite simple: if they fail to find food, they will die.

None of these options is the 'right way' to survive the winter – each has its dangers, and some may work better in certain years than in others, depending on the weather conditions that beset that particular season. Together, they present us with a wonderful array of natural phenomena, which although they may sometimes be harder to detect than at other, less testing, times of year, are nevertheless open to discovery.

Many creatures that were alive and well at the time of the winter solstice will, during the course of the season that follows, die. This may seem cruel, but it is a necessary part of the natural cycle.

For those fortunate few that do make it through this toughest time of year, opportunity beckons. As the days lengthen and eventually the temperature begins to creep up, the first signs of spring slowly start to appear. Catkins, birdsong and early snowdrops all hint at the promise of the season to come. By the spring equinox, the next great seasonal marker towards the end of March, the signs of new life will be everywhere. The onrush of April, May and June – the busiest of all our seasons, as plants and animals enter the race to reproduce – is just around the corner.

For now, as another winter solstice begins to dawn, all this activity seems a very long way off. But tomorrow the sun will begin to rise higher in the sky once again, foreshadowing the New Year to come and all the promise it will bring.

To hibernate or not to hibernate?

When it comes to surviving the winter, mammals have an inbuilt advantage over many other creatures: a furry coat to keep them warm. So although people often assume that creatures such as squirrels and badgers hibernate during the colder part of the year, in reality they do not.

In fact, of all our native mammals, only the hedgehog, dormouse and our 18 species of bat actually hibernate. Many other creatures do become less active over winter, surviving on reserves of body fat that they have built up over the summer and autumn, or, in the case of red and grey squirrels, by eating nuts that they dig up from their previously hidden stores. As a result these animals may be harder to see during these months than at other times of year, which leads to the assumption that they are hibernating.

Small mammals such as mice, voles and shrews must find vast amounts of food in winter to keep up their energy levels against the cold. Imagine being a vole and having to feed virtually all day, balancing the expenditure of energy needed to find food with the energy gained from eating it. Snow might seem to be a disaster for this little creature, yet it doesn't prevent it feeding: a vole simply burrows beneath the surface and makes tunnels down to where it can find food.

Snow and ice bring mixed fortunes for our larger mammals. For badgers, freezing conditions are a problem as these animals mainly feed on earthworms, which can be hard to find if the ground is rock-hard. So they tend to spend long periods underground, surviving on their stored fat reserves and using as little energy as possible; though not actually hibernating.

Otters, too, suffer if their watery habitat freezes over, but they solve the problem by switching their prey from fish to waterbirds such as ducks and moorhens, if necessary, and usually survive adverse conditions very well. Our largest land mammals, deer, feed by browsing the low-hanging leaves on evergreen trees or grass, which is an important part of their diet, but long periods of snow will prevent them feeding on the grass beneath.

Foxes love the snow: these mammals are opportunistic feeders, either scavenging dead birds and other animals or killing anything they find. Cold weather means more creatures die, providing lots of food for the scavenger; it also weakens many birds, so that the fox can easily pick them off. The same is true of one of our rarest and most elusive wild creatures, the Scottish wildcat, which prowls through deep, crisp snow in the Highland glens in search of pheasants and rabbits.

So what of those mammals that do choose to hibernate? Before the cold weather arrives, hedgehogs seek out a safe place to spend the winter, often

With his brick-red coat, the fox may stand out amongst the winter snows, yet he finds rich pickings at this time of year when many small mammals and birds are struggling to survive because of the cold.

buried deep inside a logpile where the temperature is fairly constant. Before doing so they feed on high-energy foods that increase their weight and build up their fat reserves, which reduces bodily heat loss and gives the animals a better chance of surviving the plummeting temperatures. The hedgehog will then reduce its metabolic rate, which lowers its body temperature from its usual 35°C (only a little below our own) to just 5–6°C, effectively shutting itself down for the whole season.

If hedgehogs are disturbed during hibernation, or if a period of mild weather during the winter period fools them into thinking spring has come, they may emerge and go off in search of food. This is often fatal, as by then their weight will have dropped below the level needed to survive, and if they cannot find plenty of food – and quickly – they will perish. The lucky ones are those that are discovered by humans and taken into care until the worst of the winter weather has passed.

> If hedgehogs are disturbed during hibernation ... they may emerge and go off in search of food. This is often fatal.

Dormice follow a similar path: in early autumn they weave a tiny nest out of bark and leaves, either in the leaf-litter on the forest floor or tucked in at the base of a hedgerow. They stay curled up in this hiding place, using their bushy tails to keep themselves warm, for up to seven months – making them the sleepiest of all our wild creatures. Having survived the worst of the winter, dormice then emerge in April or May when the weather is warmer for their brief but very active summer lives.

The mainstay of a bat's diet is flying insects – in their case, mainly moths, flies and midges – so once the chill winds of autumn begin to blow, and the insects disappear, they are unable to feed. But unlike insect-eating birds (such as swallows and swifts) that can fly to Africa, bats cannot travel long distances; so their only option for surviving our winter is to hibernate. They hide away in roosts: sometimes in caves or the hollows of trees, but often in our buildings – barns, sheds and even the attics of houses. If you do come across bats roosting on your property, make sure you don't disturb them – it is against the law to do so, as it is potentially fatal for the creatures.

On a fine day in April (or occasionally as early as March if the weather is warm enough), these bats will begin to emerge from hibernation to hunt for insects once again.

Unseasonably mild winter weather can fool hibernating hedgehogs into thinking spring has come early; but if they cannot find enough food they will starve to death.

The stay-at-home birds' survival guide

Britain is a nation of bird-lovers. We have become so attached to the robins, tits and blackbirds visiting our bird tables that we often think of them as 'our' birds, even though their habit of roving and visiting several gardens during the course of a day means that we do in fact share them with our neighbours.

People often assume that small birds perish in winter because of the cold. In fact the fall in temperature is rarely the direct cause of any creature's demise; the real reason is that if they are unable to maintain their energy levels through feeding, their weight will drop below that which is necessary for them to survive.

So, many of these creatures really do depend on us for their survival. At this time of year, if these birds do not eat, they will almost certainly die, especially during very cold weather. During the shortest days of winter, a blue tit has only a few hours of daylight in which it must find up to one-third of its body weight in food.

A wide range of species, mainly those that evolved in woodland and farmland habitats, now regularly visit our gardens. Bird tables stocked with seed and peanut feeders hung around the garden – not forgetting the regular supply of fresh water in bird baths for drinking and bathing – offer a lifeline.

Tits, finches, starlings and sparrows are the most regular visitors to hanging feeders, while blackbirds, thrushes, robins and dunnocks forage on the ground beneath. Other visitors may include great spotted and green woodpeckers, and two species of finch; the black, red and yellow goldfinch, and the streaky green and black siskin. For the latter two species, the widespread surge in feeding birds has enabled them to extend their breeding range and increase their numbers.

For these birds, which often struggle to survive, garden feeding means they can now get through even the harshest winter. The Big Freeze of 1962–63 hit long-tailed tits in particular hard because these birds eat tiny insects which were scarce during the very cold weather. As a result, up to 90 per cent of the UK population of long-tailed tits were dead by the following spring. But during the winter of 2009–10, which in some parts of Britain was the coldest since the Big Freeze, many more of these tiny birds survived thanks to their newfound ability to cling onto seed-feeders and consume their contents.

Natural food – in the form of seeds and tiny insects – is of course still available in winter, and many birds, including tits and finches, do forage in the wider countryside. Unlike in the breeding season, when males fend off their rivals and closely guard their mates, these small birds become far more sociable at this time of year, forming tight-knit flocks so they can search for food together. Flocking has two huge advantages over going it alone: first, it gives the birds more

Blue tits may be small, but they always manage to hold their own at bird feeders, ensuring that they get plenty of energy-giving seeds and nuts to help them survive the long, cold winter nights.

opportunity to find food, but it is also the best way to stay safe, as numerous pairs of eyes and ears make it easier to spot danger.

In woodland, the commonest birds to be found are often the tits. These usually include the largest member of the family, the great tit, with its distinctive green and yellow plumage, black head, white cheeks and smart black stripe running down the centre of its breast; and the smaller blue tit, whose blue and yellow plumage is equally distinctive. They may also be joined by the more monochrome coal and marsh tits, which can be told apart by the coal tit's distinctive white patch on the back of its head.

Other species that often join forces with tit flocks include long-tailed tits, which despite their name are not true tits. These charming little birds are easy to identify, as their plump bodies with long tails sticking out behind give them the appearance of flying lollipops! Our smallest bird, the green and yellow goldcrest, may also accompany these birds, as does the pugnacious nuthatch with his distinctive black 'bandit mask' across his face, the tiny, mouse-like treecreeper, and occasionally a much scarcer species, the lesser spotted woodpecker. Only the size of a sparrow, our smallest woodpecker is very easy to overlook as he tags along with the other birds.

In more open countryside, where there are fields and hedgerows, seed-eating birds such as finches, buntings and sparrows gather, foraging on the ground for waste seeds and grains, or perching on plants such as docks or teasels to pick out the seeds. However, in the past few decades industrial farming methods have greatly reduced the amount of seed and grain available: either because stubble fields have been replaced with sterile prairies of winter wheat, or because the wild plants that used to grow around the edges of the fields have been ploughed up in the quest for even greater efficiency of food production.

Until recently, farmland bird species such as the handsome, black-headed reed bunting and the yellowhammer – whose golden-yellow plumage makes it one of our most striking birds – would never have ventured away from their usual habitat and into gardens, but the shortage of food in the wider countryside, combined with its availability in gardens, means they both now regularly do so.

For these resident birds, staying put during the winter, rather than migrating to warmer climes, has advantages and disadvantages. In a mild winter, with plenty of food available, they do well; when there is a prolonged cold snap, or worse still a hard winter with ice and snow for weeks or even months, they do very badly indeed. Of course they have no choice: both as individuals and species they have evolved to stay put, so they no longer have the ability to migrate long distances. Instead, like other non-migratory animals, they have to use every means they can to find food, stay warm and survive until spring.

Flocking enables the birds to find food more easily because there are more birds searching for it, but it is also the best way to stay safe.

Teasles offer a delicious feast for goldfinches, who use their thin, needle-sharp bills to prise the tiny seeds out of these plants.

Winter hide and seek

Insects, reptiles and amphibians also stay put for the winter, and so they too face a real battle in this cold season. They cannot migrate to warmer climes, and unlike many of our resident birds and mammals, they struggle to find food during the unforgiving winter months.

Insects, as well as other invertebrates, such as spiders, woodlice, snails and slugs, tend to hide away in damp places such as rockeries and woodpiles, and there they lie dormant during the winter season. We sometimes come across them: either inside the warmth of our own homes (a favourite place for spiders) or more commonly in our garden sheds, garages and other outbuildings, which are ideal places for these small creatures to hide away from predators, and from the cold.

During the winter you may also come across butterflies, often in the dark corner of a shed or garage. Their wings are closed, they do not move when touched, and so to all intents and purposes they look as if they are dead. But in fact they are in a state of dormancy, which enables them to survive until the warmer spring days arrive and they can fly again in search of nectar from your garden flowers.

Four species of butterfly traditionally overwinter as adults in Britain: the small tortoiseshell, peacock, comma and brimstone – although during the past decade they have been joined by a fifth, the red admiral, which has taken advantage of a run of mild winters to stay put here instead of migrating south. Lately, spells of mild weather in late winter mean that we often see these overwintering butterflies flitting about in March, or even January or February. Unfortunately, if they do emerge this early in the year it is unlikely that they will survive for very long, as a returning cold snap quickly kills off blossom and early flowers, destroying any nectar the insects need to feed on.

Two other groups of animals that hibernate are reptiles and amphibians. We have six species of reptile in Britain: three snakes – the adder, grass snake and smooth snake; and three lizards – the common and sand lizards, and the slow worm. All of these hibernate during the winter, either tucked away in a logpile or compost heap or under foliage on their native heaths.

All our native amphibians – frogs, toads and newts – also hibernate, often in damp areas of our gardens where you may unwittingly discover them while digging up the soil in preparation for the coming spring. Again, if you do disturb any hibernating creatures, it is important that you always put them back where you found them and cover them over so they can continue to rest until the warmer temperatures naturally wake them from their slumber.

During the past decade the red admiral has taken advantage of a run of mild winters to stay put here instead of migrating south.

A seven-spot ladybird soaks up the sun's rays in an empty acorn cup in spring, warming up after a winter spent in hibernation.

Weary winter plants

Plants, of course, cannot migrate, and are generally dormant at this time of year, as temperatures are too low for them to grow. Yet that does not mean that nothing is happening amongst them: our woods and hedgerows may appear quiet and lifeless, but extraordinary biological processes are going on all the while in order to prepare for the year ahead, which involves shutting down all growing and reproductive mechanisms in order to save energy.

By the time winter arrives, many flowering plants have already done all the hard work required to guarantee that they will re-emerge in spring. Annuals – those plants that live for just one growing season and die off each autumn – have ensured continuity of their species by setting seed in a final swansong (see page 219). Many perennial plants, such as snowdrops, wild garlic, wild daffodils and bluebells, prepare for dormancy by storing energy underground in their bulbs. Outside the growing season, from autumn onwards, these plants accumulate food reserves in these bulbs, which continue to grow, but as spring approaches the plants switch into their reproductive state and shoots grow upwards from the top of the bulb, pushing through the soil and up towards the light. This change in activity is triggered by rising temperatures and increased day length as winter gives way to spring.

> By the time winter arrives, many flowering plants have already done all the hard work required to guarantee that they will re-emerge in spring.

Trees have two very different strategies that they use to survive the winter, depending on the species. Deciduous trees such as oak, ash and beech drop their leaves in autumn to preserve their water content, which would otherwise be lost through their large surface area during a process known as transpiration. Shedding leaves also enables the trees to conserve energy during cold months when they would be unable to grow or produce seeds or fruit. In contrast, evergreen species such as the Scots pine and yew do not shed their leaves, which have evolved to have far less surface area than those of deciduous trees to prevent water loss. These thin, waxy leaves are commonly known as 'needles'.

As spring approaches, the first signs of life return to our deciduous trees, as initially the buds and then the young leaves begin to appear, signalling that the season of cold is over at last.

A classic winter scene in the Brecon Beacons in Wales, one of our most scenically beautiful national parks.

Life at the top

Whatever the season, no native landscape can be as hostile and difficult a habitat as the mountaintops of the Scottish Highlands, especially the Cairngorm plateau – the windiest, coldest and toughest place in Britain. It is hard to believe that any living creature could possibly survive here, especially in winter – and yet some can, and do.

These magnificent sites are some of our last truly wild locations: vast plateaux and peaks covered for much of the year in snow, and although there are not many species that choose to live all year round on the high tops, the ones that do stay put are spectacular and exciting in their appearance and behaviour.

Three creatures in particular that live on the mountaintops in winter have a unique and attractive feature in common: they are the only British creatures that turn white in winter. They do so, of course, to camouflage themselves in this snowy environment. The first is the ptarmigan (pronounced with a silent 'p', as in 'tar-mig-en'). The name comes from a Scottish Gaelic word meaning 'croaker' and refers to the species' rasping call. The ptarmigan is unique amongst British birds for its three different plumages during the year: brown in spring to match the heather, grey in autumn to blend in with the lichen-covered, boulder-strewn landscape, and white in winter. This enables the ptarmigan to avoid being spotted by predators, including the sharp-eyed golden eagle. Ptarmigan survive in winter by feeding on berries and plant shoots, and withstand the harsh weather by digging holes in the snow where they hide until the storms are over.

Next are two mammals – stoats and mountain hares – which both turn white in winter, each for very different reasons. Stoats turn completely white apart from the black tip of the tail (and are known as 'ermine' – their fur was famously used to adorn the robes of medieval monarchs). By changing colour in winter, the stoats are able to blend in to their surroundings and so sneak up on their prey. The mountain hare also turns virtually completely white to become less visible to its predator: the aforementioned stoat. Thus Nature evens up the chances between these two creatures.

The ptarmigan, mountain hare and stoat can all be hard to spot in winter as a result of their excellent camouflage, but another animal is much easier to see: the feral herd of reindeer that lives near the summit of the mountain of Cairngorm itself, in the centre of the Cairngorms National Park.

During and just after the last Ice Age, up until about 8,000 years ago, reindeer were found throughout much of upland Britain, but as the climate warmed up they became extinct. In 1952, a Swedish reindeer herder brought a small herd

The mountain hare is one of the toughest of all our wild creatures, surviving through the long winter on the mountainsides of the Cairngorm plateau in the Scottish Highlands. It takes on a pure-white garb in winter to camouflage itself against the snow and protect itself from predators.

to the Cairngorms, and during the following decades numbers increased to the current count of about 150 animals.

Although they are not technically wild, and are looked after and given food by herders from the Cairngorm Reindeer Centre, these classic Christmas animals still make a fine sight as they forage for food amongst the snow.

However, the most glorious sight in a clear winter sky is the soaring form of the mighty golden eagle – the true monarch of the mountains. One of our largest and most magnificent birds of prey, with a wingspan of over two metres, it also has two feathered talons with which to seize its quarry, and a heavy bill capable of tearing flesh from bone.

Golden eagles spend the winter roving long distances over their vast upland territory, in search of food. Sometimes they will hunt and kill their prey – red grouse, ptarmigan and mountain hare are their favourite foods – but they will also often simply seek out the corpses of dead animals such as deer. These provide a very easy meal with the minimal expenditure of energy for the bird itself; vitally important at this time of year, because if the eagle uses too much energy hunting in vain, it risks dying of starvation. The eagle's incredible eyesight – up to ten times more powerful than ours – is a key factor in enabling it to spot a dead or dying creature, or potential prey, from a distance of several miles away.

Resilient raptors

Of all our birds, one group stands head and shoulders above the others in terms of strength, power and sheer magnificence: our birds of prey – or raptors, as they are often known. From the tiny merlin (our smallest falcon, not much larger than a blackbird) to the white-tailed eagle, whose 2.5-metre wingspan is the largest of any British bird, they deserve their central place in our history and mythology. Eagles, hawks and falcons often appear on coats of arms or as emblems of power (such as the Roman Empire), and the practice of falconry – using a bird of prey to hunt quarry – goes back to medieval times.

For centuries, though, any bird 'red in tooth and claw' was regarded by humans as a mortal enemy, especially to gamekeepers, who resorted to trapping, shooting and killing them in order to protect gamebirds such as pheasants and red grouse. Sadly, a handful of landowners and gamekeepers still illegally trap and kill birds of prey, but fortunately this is far less widespread than it used to be.

Once our commonest bird of prey, but now unfortunately in decline, kestrels are known for their habit of hovering above verges, though in winter they tend to hunt from a fixed perch on a fence, pole or telegraph wire, as hovering uses too much of their precious energy reserves.

Sparrowhawks and buzzards are sometimes seen soaring, especially on fine days, while peregrines and merlins hunt over coastal estuaries and freshwater marshes, along with marsh and hen harriers. Winter days may be short, but they are a good time for these birds to hunt, as their prey species such as waders and ducks flock together to find food, so can be found in large numbers.

Of all Britain's birds of prey success stories, the red kite is the most heartwarming. This elegant raptor, with its brick-red plumage, long wings and deeply forked tail, was driven to the brink of extinction here at the turn of the twentieth century through sustained and deliberate persecution, surviving only in a few remote and wooded valleys in mid-Wales. But since the 1980s, red kites have been reintroduced into parts of central and southern England and Scotland. The results are amazing: within a few years they became one of the commonest, most visible birds in places such as the Chilterns, where they often hunt over the M40. They even visit gardens, swooping down with their acrobatic antics to grab chicken legs and other food put out by householders.

Winter is a great time to get good and prolonged views of kites, as this is when they take advantage of farmers ploughing up the earth by following behind to pick up earthworms – one of their favourite foods! Watching a kite as it hangs in the air on its broad, narrow wings is a magnificent sight – and one that thanks to their renewed success is something more and more of us are able to witness.

Of all our birds, one group stands head and shoulders above the others in terms of strength, power and sheer magnificence: our birds of prey.

OPPOSITE: The beautiful and elegant red kite has been brought back from the brink of extinction in Britain and now is one of the most visible birds in many parts of the country, particularly in the winter months.

FOLLOWING PAGES: Winter is a time when birds need their wits about them while hunting. Mute swans scan the frozen countryside for food as they fly above a flock of young common cranes.

Wise owls of winter

Owls are amongst our most mysterious and much-loved birds: partly because of their predominantly nocturnal habits, but also because they have a central place in British mythology and folklore. They are anthropomorphic birds, too; they have always been presented as wise in legend and literature, which is perhaps because their forward-facing eyes make them appear more human in character than other birds. Five species of owl – tawny, barn, little, long-eared and short-eared – are resident in Britain; while a sixth species, the Arctic-dwelling snowy owl, is a rare visitor during the autumn and winter months, usually to the northern and western islands of Scotland.

The commonest British owl is also one of the most nocturnal: the tawny owl (sometimes known as the brown owl because of the colour of its plumage). After hunting for small rodents such as mice and voles during the hours of darkness, tawny owls spend the daylight hours asleep, usually roosting in a hollow trunk of a mature tree such as an oak. Their presence may be revealed by the sight of small birds 'mobbing' the unwelcome predator in their midst, in order to try to drive it away – a strategy that looks risky but often works.

> Five species of owl – tawny, barn, little, long-eared and short-eared – are resident in Britain; while a sixth species, the Arctic-dwelling snowy owl, is a rare visitor.

The barn owl (also sometimes known as the screech owl) is easier to see than the tawny owl as it hunts both at dawn and dusk, its ghostly white appearance in the half light making it easy to spot and to identify. Barn owls hunt using their incredibly acute hearing to listen for the tell-tale rustling of voles and mice. High-pressure weather systems bringing crisp, cold winter days with no wind are ideal for hunting; these owls struggle to locate their prey during strong winds as this impairs their ability to hear the tiny movements on which they depend to pinpoint their victim. Snow is bad news for barn owls, as it covers up their prey – though the following breeding season often brings a bonanza as voles are able to breed beneath it, meaning there are usually plenty around after a hard winter. Rain is even more of a hindrance, as the owls' soft flight feathers, which enable them to fly so silently, easily become waterlogged.

The smallest British owl, the aptly-named little owl, is often seen during the day, perched on the stumps of trees, fence posts or roofs; though its small size

The barn owl's heart-shaped face enables it to focus and concentrate the tiny sounds of voles and mice as they scurry beneath the snow. In this way the owl has a better chance of locating and catching them.

can make it hard to locate. During the winter months this owl hunts for small mammals and birds, which it seizes in its powerful claws. The scientific name of the little owl, *Athene noctua*, refers to the Greek goddess Athena, who is always depicted carrying a small owl.

The two 'eared' owls – long-eared and short-eared – have very different lifestyles from one another. The former is the most nocturnal of all our owls, though they do gather in daytime roosts, often in dense blackthorn bushes. The short-eared owl is much more obliging, as it hunts during the day. In autumn and winter we sometimes get invasions of short-eared owls from continental Europe, which come over the North Sea and English Channel because of a shortage of food in their breeding areas, either caused by bad weather or simply because vole populations run in cycles, with highs and lows depending on the year. In some winters there may be groups of up to a dozen short-eared owls hunting over rough grassland almost anywhere in southern Britain.

The mighty oak

No tree better symbolises the British, and in particular the English, landscape than the oak. It can be found across much of lowland Britain, along roadsides and in the middle of fields, or in magnificent ancient woodlands. It is easy to identify, both from a distance, thanks to its classic shape and thick trunk and branches, and close-up, because of its very distinctive wavy-edged leaves and, in autumn, acorns.

Oaks are one of our longest-lived trees: many are at least 500 years old, while a few specimens have survived here since before the Norman Conquest, making them over 1,000 years old – not quite as old, admittedly, as the Fortingall Yew (see page 48), but nevertheless pretty impressive!

The longevity of the English oak means that over many millennia it's become home to a wide range of different insects. This means that the oak is also an excellent provider of food for birds and mammals, including jays and squirrels, which eat the acorns, and deer, which browse the young leaves in spring. A large, mature oak also provides shelter from bad weather, a place to roost and sleep, and, of course, a place to nest for many different kinds of bird, from warblers to woodpeckers.

During the winter it might appear that the oak tree is lifeless, yet nothing could be further from the truth: beneath the bark there are millions of insects, feeding, pupating and surviving the cold weather in this wooden haven. And as winter edges towards spring, look out for the sticky buds that appear near the end of each twig: signs of life in the season to come.

In winter deciduous trees such as the oak survive by losing their leaves, which enables them to preserve water and avoid drying out.

Wetland visitors

When we think of migrating birds, those that usually come to mind are the ones who leave us in autumn, having visited us during the summer months. Birds such as the swallow, house martin and cuckoo arrive in spring, breed and raise their families with us during the summer, and then head south in autumn to spend the winter in Africa. However, there is also another important group of migrants who travel vast distances to be with us and whom we tend to overlook. These are our winter visitors: ducks, geese and swans – collectively known as wildfowl – and wading birds.

Britain provides an important winter home to millions of these birds, which gather together to create some of the most memorable natural spectacles of all. These birds head to our shores from their breeding grounds in the north, the west and the east, such as Arctic Canada, Iceland and Greenland, Scandinavia and Siberia. During the summer months, when there is almost 24-hour daylight and

In winter, Britain provides a welcome home for many visiting ducks, including small dabbling ones such as the teal, who congregate in low-lying wetlands in the southern and western parts of the country.

plenty of food, these countries are the ideal place to raise their young. But as summer slips into autumn and the nights rapidly begin to draw in, these birds head south and west in search of a milder climate.

To get here, the birds fly over the North Atlantic and the North Sea, travelling several hundred or even several thousand miles to reach Britain. They often – especially geese, and Bewick's and whooper swans – travel in family parties, with the parents leading their offspring on their first ever migratory voyage. Unlike songbirds, which migrate under cover of darkness, wildfowl usually travel by day and may be seen arriving from late October or November onwards at well-known sites such as the Ouse Washes in East Anglia, the Severn Estuary, and Caerlaverock on the Solway Firth.

British winters may often be cold and bleak, but they are a picnic compared with the conditions in these birds' Arctic homes at the same time of year. If they stayed put, they would surely perish, for the winter months so far north are a time of freezing temperatures, bitter winds and almost permanent darkness, where very few living creatures are able to survive. Britain is not only further south, with longer hours of daylight even in the middle of winter, but its climate is also heavily influenced by the proximity of the Atlantic Ocean and the warming Gulf Stream. So even though the thermometer dips below freezing, and there may be snow and ice, our coastal estuaries enable vast flocks of migratory birds to find plenty of food through the winter. The hungry birds survive by feeding at low tide. As the waters rise and cover their feeding areas, they simply gather together in huge flocks to sit out the change of tide.

Coastal sites are not the only places where these migratory birds gather, Britain has many other large bodies of water, such as lakes, gravel pits and reservoirs, which are the winter home to large flocks of ducks. The key species are wigeon, teal and shoveler – all dabbling ducks, which feed by 'up-ending'; and tufted duck and pochard – known as diving ducks, which plunge beneath the surface of the water to find their food.

There may also be smaller numbers of goosander – one of our largest ducks, with a distinctive thin bill, dark green head and creamy plumage; the goldeneye – sporting their eponymous bright-yellow eye; and the rare and beautiful smew, whose snow-white plumage lined with black led one observer to describe them as 'looking like a cracked vase that has been glued back together again'.

These wintering birds arrive in late autumn or early winter and remain until March or even April. During the last weeks of their stay, they often indulge in elaborate courtship behaviour, the males performing intricate displays in front of deeply unimpressed females in order to win back their affection. Once they have renewed their pair bond they will then fly together back to their breeding grounds, and begin the long and arduous process of raising a family once again.

Even though the thermometer dips below freezing … our coastal estuaries enable vast flocks of migratory birds to find plenty of food through the winter.

Ponds through the seasons

A pond in winter may appear to be deserted, but in the cold waters life goes on. Frogs overwinter alongside larvae and insects such as dragonflies, waiting for the weather to warm up when they can re-emerge. In early spring frogs will lay frogspawn, newts will lay eggs and hoverflies begin to visit. In summer, the pond is abuzz with activity as eggs hatch and a new generation of insects and other wildlife, including ducks, take to the water. As the autumn chill descends, the cycle ends and the pond's wildlife prepares for a quiet winter and the wait for warmer weather once more.

Predatory peregrines

There can be few more spectacular sights on a winter's day than a flock of thousands of wading birds such as dunlin or knot taking to the air as one to evade a hunting peregrine falcon – the fastest living creature on the planet.

At first sight this might appear an unequal contest: surely the power, might and skill of the peregrine will win every time? Yet it doesn't work out that way: in fact, like all relationships between predators and their prey, whether lions hunting antelopes on the African plains or a polar bear stalking seals on the Arctic ice, the situation is balanced on a knife-edge.

As with all birds in winter, the waders must feed at every opportunity, otherwise their body weight will plummet to dangerously low levels and they will lose the battle to survive. So to try to avoid being caught by predators

The peregrine falcon is the fastest creature on the planet, able to reach speeds of almost 250 mph in its incredible hunting dive, known as a 'stoop'.

they gather in flocks, ensuring that thousands, rather than just one pair, of eyes are watching out for danger.

Even when these birds sleep in their high-tide roost, they frequently open their eyes to check for any predators passing overhead. They also have a special membrane that flashes white across their eyes when they are asleep, giving the impression that they are awake and alert to danger even when they are snoozing.

When a predator such as a peregrine does suddenly appear, cutting through the chill winter's air like a knife, any bird that spots it will immediately utter a sharp, penetratingly loud alarm call. This is the signal for it and all its neighbours to take to the air. A moving target is harder for the peregrine to hit than a sitting one; and the twisting and turning of the flock – appearing almost as a single organism governed by one giant brain – confuses the hunter, because virtually as soon as it has fixed its eyes upon a target, that bird has disappeared into the rest of the swirling mass.

To us, it appears as if the birds are working together as a team to foil their attacker. The truth is both simpler and more elegant: each bird is doing all it can to avoid being picked out, which means staying as close as it can to the birds immediately around it, and therefore to the rest of the flock. Any birds that lag behind – either through injury or inexperience – will soon be picked off, so it makes sense to stay with the main body of birds.

From the peregrine's point of view, the best strategy is to try to ignore this confusing mass of birds and simply target one lone individual – ideally one on the edge. Once it has done so, it will go into the famous 'stoop' – an incredibly fast aerial pursuit reaching speeds of at least 180 miles per hour, and possibly far faster.

> Any birds that lag behind – either through injury or inexperience – will soon be picked off, so it makes sense to stay with the main body of birds.

A flock of starlings gathers before landing at their winter roost, but is disturbed by a hunting peregrine falcon.

As the peregrine approaches its target, it suddenly brakes by lifting up its wings and bringing its feet forward in preparation for the actual attack. With one practised movement it extends its razor-sharp talons and grabs the unfortunate wader, squeezing the life out of it in a fraction of a second, before returning to its perch to pluck and eat its prey. For the victim, life is over; for the peregrine, success means vital energy, which it, too, needs in order to survive the winter months.

Britain's oldest tree

In the corner of a churchyard in Fortingall, a quiet little village in the highlands of Perthshire, Scotland, stands Britain's most ancient tree. Were it not separated from the rest of the churchyard by a low stone wall, you might easily dismiss it as just another gnarled and crooked yew tree.

But the Fortingall Yew is more than any old tree: it is the *oldest* tree in Britain, and possibly in the whole of Europe. It was certainly alive when Christ was born and when Julius Caesar invaded Britain, and it may have been very old even then. Its age has been estimated at between 2,500 and 5,000 years, which makes it not just the oldest tree, but also the oldest living thing in Britain.

Yew trees have been important and valuable trees since time immemorial. Their timber has always been highly prized: it is heavy and dense but also very flexible, and was used to make longbows during the Hundred Years War between England and France. Today it is still valued as a wood for making furniture. The trees are often found in churchyards, and this siting is no coincidence. Most of Britain's older Christian churches were built on former pagan sites, where our ancestors gathered to worship long before the birth of Christ. Thanks to their extraordinary longevity and evergreen foliage, yew trees were considered to be symbols of long life, and so they were often deliberately planted at these special pagan places and remained when these were replaced by Christian churches.

Yews are fascinating for many reasons other than their long life. Though not one of our largest trees – most yews grow between 10 and 20 metres in height – it does have other qualities, not least the fact that many parts of the tree are highly poisonous. The leaves, for instance, are toxic to most domestic livestock, especially horses and cattle. This may also explain why yews survived better inside churchyards than out in the wider countryside, where farmers would have uprooted them to protect their animals.

Surprisingly, the part of the yew that you might expect to be poisonous – the bright red, wax-like berries that stud the dark foliage like decorations on a Christmas tree from early autumn – are not. A wide range of birds, especially thrushes, blackbirds and finches, feed up for winter on these berries and then disperse the hard seeds via their droppings, enabling the yew tree to spread further afield.

The dense, dark interior of the yew tree allows tiny insects to survive amongst the leaves and bark in even the coldest winters by creating a microclimate of its own, where temperatures remain constant. These insects in turn attract two of our smallest species of bird, the wren and the goldcrest, which forage unseen beneath the tree's canopy, picking off tiny insects with their needle-thin bills.

The dense, dark interior of the yew tree allows tiny insects to survive amongst the leaves and bark in even the coldest winters.

As one of our three native conifers – the Scots pine and the juniper are the other two – the yew has evolved to withstand the very worst of the British winter weather. The leaves are, like those of most conifers, narrow and flattened to avoid losing water through evaporation, and the conical shape of the tree means that snow slips off the branches rather than settling and causing damage.

Like other conifers, the yew also contains resins in its sap – a kind of natural antifreeze – that prevent ice crystals forming and damaging the delicate cells inside the tree during cold winters. All in all, with such a combination of natural defences and usefulness to man, it is hardly surprising that the yew tree is such an incredible survivor.

Yews are famed for their extraordinary longevity, and may live to several thousand years old.

Winter on the wane

As the winter drags on from January into February, we look hopefully for signs of spring – the early evidence that the seasons are changing and life is beginning to return to our bleak, wintry landscape.

The appearance of the snowdrop is a classic sign that winter is, if not exactly over, at least on the wane, and spring may be around the corner. If we search every nook of our gardens, parks, woods and churchyards, we'll find that tell-tale sign of the first green shoots that come before those delicate yet hardy snow-white blooms.

Traditionally snowdrops are expected to begin flowering on Candlemas Day (2 February), but they can bloom at any time between January and late March, depending on how far north or south they are, and whether or not it has been a mild or hard winter.

Given that most flowering plants won't appear until March or April, how is it that snowdrops are able to bloom so early? One reason is that they remain in the ground as perennial bulbs, which enables them to store their energy during the dormant winter period, so they are prepared and able to rapidly take advantage of higher temperatures as soon as they arrive.

> The appearance of the snowdrop is a classic sign that winter is, if not exactly over, at least on the wane, and spring may be around the corner.

Snowdrops also have leaves with specially hardened tips which enable the plant to push through the frost-hardened ground up into the open air. When the flowers appear there are very few insects around to pollinate them, so the plants usually rely on bulb division to colonise new areas across the woodland floor. However, occasionally an early bumblebee – often a queen, as these are usually the first to emerge in spring – will pollinate the plants, enabling them to set seed later in the year.

Two other early-flowering beauties soon follow snowdrops: the lesser celandine and the primrose. The lesser celandine is a delicate-looking little flower – a splash of custard yellow amongst its green foliage – yet despite its

Snowdrops are, appropriately, one of the very first flowers to appear in a new year, often blooming when there is still frost and snow on the ground.

frail appearance it can often be seen as early as February. Its flowers open when the sun shines and then close when it goes behind a cloud, so that on sunny days the woodland floor is carpeted with them, while on dull days they seem to vanish.

The primrose (its name comes from the Latin *'prima rosa'*, which means 'first flower') is one of our best-known and most-loved spring flowers. The first primroses usually appear in the southwest of England, where the mild climate allows them to bloom in profusion along the hedgerows of Devon and Cornwall.

Another flower that may appear in the middle of winter doesn't resemble a flower at all. Catkins hang from the branches of hazel trees very early in the year: these rely on the wind to spread their pollen, so it is a real advantage that they appear before there are leaves on other trees, which otherwise would block the grains of pollen from spreading.

Another classic sign of spring arriving can be seen in our garden ponds and other bodies of water. Frogspawn may appear any time from New Year onwards in mild winters, though if there is very harsh weather it may be delayed by several weeks or even months. These clusters of jelly are pretty tough – even if the surface of the water freezes over, the frogspawn beneath will sometimes manage to survive, though if freezing conditions persist it will usually die off.

LEFT: Providing a welcome splash of colour as winter draws to a close, the primrose lifts up its cheery petals even in snow.

OPPOSITE: Frogs are surprisingly tough, and lay their characteristic clumps of eggs – known as frogspawn – long before spring has officially arrived.

The sounds of spring

In the middle of winter, in the cities or the countryside, you may be surprised to hear a snatch of birdsong. And yet as the days pass and the evenings get fractionally lighter, the chorus begins to build, until by March there is a cacophony of sound at dawn and dusk.

Male birds sing at this time of year for two reasons: to repel rival males from their breeding territory, and to find a mate (or in some cases, mates). As the breeding season approaches, such is the competition for both the best territories and the best females that a male songbird will often sing throughout most of the daylight hours, only stopping from time to time to find food in order to gain the energy to continue singing.

This is a risky business: not only does the bird use up valuable energy by singing, but his conspicuousness as he sings away on a prominent perch (the best place for both rivals and potential lovers to see him) makes him an easy target for a predator such as a sparrowhawk. And yet he continues to sing, for if he fails to hold a territory, win a mate and reproduce he may never get another chance – after all, the natural lifespan of most small birds is only one or two years.

Because there is little or no foliage on the trees and bushes at this time of year, you can often see the birds as well as hear them, which provides the perfect conditions in which to learn their songs and calls. Typical early starters, soon after the turn of the New Year, are song and mistle thrushes – which can be told apart by the more repetitive nature of the song thrush's phrasing, as well as the bird's smaller size and mid-brown, rather than pale grey-brown, plumage.

But of all the birds that sing at this time of year, the robin is the best known. Indeed, robins may have been singing throughout the autumn and winter months as, unlike the vast majority of birds, they hold a territory at this time of year in order to defend their food supply, and they need to sing to repel rivals.

Soon afterwards, usually by February or the beginning of March, these early singers are joined by blue and great tits – the latter singing their famous 'tea-cher, tea-cher' song, with the emphasis on the second syllable. Wrens sing their loud, trilling descant, dunnocks their rather tuneless warble, and blackbirds their more pleasant-sounding, deep and fluty song. They are soon joined by the finches: the loud and exuberant chaffinch, whose song (a series of notes that speed up towards the end of the phrase) has been described as having the rhythm of a fast-bowler at cricket; the greenfinch, with his wheezy trills; and the delicate tinkling of the goldfinch.

By mid-to-late March the first returning migrants join the chorus: the classic two-note song of the chiffchaff – a small, olive-coloured warbler – echoes

> Such is the competition for both the best territories and the best females that a male songbird will often sing throughout most of the daylight hours.

PREVIOUS PAGES: Squirrels never hibernate, so you might be lucky enough to see our native red squirrel at this time of year.

OPPOSITE: The male greenfinch sings its heart out, hoping that its wheezy trills will attract an interested female.

through woods and gardens, while another warbler, the larger, greyer blackcap, follows soon afterwards. The blackcap sings a more melodious tune, rather reminiscent of that of a blackbird but an octave higher in pitch, and may also be heard in rural gardens and along the edges of woods. These resident birds and early arrivals then have the stage to themselves until spring proper arrives, and with it summer visitors such as the willow warbler and cuckoo.

Another early spring sound is not strictly song at all, though it performs the same function. Woodpeckers – especially the starling-sized great spotted – begin to drum early in the year. The male perches on the side of a tree trunk or on a thick branch, using his sharp claws and specially stiffened tail feathers to help him hold on. He then batters his sharp, pointed bill against the wood up to forty times a second – a blur to the eye.

It is impossible for the human ear to distinguish the individual sounds he is making; only when a film or sound recording of the bird is slowed down does the complexity of the drumming become clear. His powerful neck muscles and a spongy padding around the base of its bill act like shock absorbers on a car, preventing him getting a headache!

For all these birds, even though winter may still be with us, the breeding season has now well and truly begun. We will only be able to measure their success later in the year, once they have completed their breeding cycle.

It is impossible for the human ear to distinguish the individual sounds the woodpecker is making; only when a film or sound recording of the bird is slowed down does the complexity of the drumming become clear.

The great spotted woodpecker will often start to drum in late winter, banging its bill repeatedly against the trunk or branch of a tree to repel rival males and attract a mate.

Early breeding birds

Although many birds wait until spring to breed, a few get a headstart in late winter. Some, like the wood pigeon and collared dove, are simply opportunists: provided they can find enough food they will nest in any month of the year – even the middle of winter! Others, though, always breed early, including two members of the crow family – the rook and raven – the grey heron and crossbills.

The sight of a flock of rooks returning to their old nests in the tops of tall trees early in the New Year is an iconic one in many villages up and down the country. Rooks are sociable creatures and love to nest in tightly packed colonies, cheek-by-jowl with one another. From January onwards they can be seen in the bare twigs, making emergency repairs to last year's nest or, if heavy autumn and winter gales have blown the nest down, building a new one altogether.

Rooks breed so early because they feed themselves and their young mainly on earthworms and other soil-dwelling invertebrates. When the ground is wet in late winter and early spring it is easier for them to find these in the soft earth; later on, as the ground hardens, worms are harder to find. It is in these months that rooks look elsewhere for nutrients, often in farmers' fields. In fact, the familiar farmers' 'scarecrow' was not designed to frighten the usually solitary carrion crows, but to stop large flocks of rooks from eating precious grain – it should really be called a 'scarerook'!

Ravens, the largest member of the crow family, are also early nesters; again, the reason for this is diet-related, for ravens are mainly scavengers of carrion, and late winter provides plenty of corpses of birds and mammals that have died from starvation. Ravens often nest high on a mountainside, hence the prevalence of place names in Britain such as 'Ravenscraig', derived from 'raven's crag'. Like other large and impressive birds, ravens gave rise to a wealth of myths and folklore – including the superstition that they carry the souls of the dead to the afterlife – a belief that may have taken hold because ravens were a common sight on battlefields in the aftermath of medieval conflicts.

Like rooks and ravens, grey herons build their huge nests out of sticks and in communal colonies known as 'heronries'. They too breed early because of their diet: which in this case consists of fish and frogs, which are easier to catch early in the year before the surfaces of ponds and streams become clogged with a layer of duckweed. However, in hard winters herons need to delay nesting as they are unable to find food through a layer of ice.

Various species of crossbill are also able to nest early in the year because of the unique adaptation that gives them their name. The upper and lower parts

Rooks love to nest in colonies high up in the canopies of woodland trees, where their nests are easily visible in the bare winter branches.

of their beak (known as mandibles) cross over one another instead of fitting neatly together as those of other birds do, which enables them to prise the tiny seeds out of the cones of conifers such as pines, a food source that, unlike insects, is available all year round. So in the Caledonian pine forests of the Scottish Highlands, the endemic Scottish crossbill – the only British bird species found nowhere else in the world – may have chicks in their nests as early as February, when there is still a thick layer of snow on the ground beneath.

This time of year also sees the peak of one of the strangest forms of behaviour of all – lekking – which is carried out by two large gamebirds: the capercaillie and black grouse. The word 'lek' derives from a Swedish one meaning 'play' or 'court', and the performance does have something theatrical about it.

These two species are amongst the largest and most striking of all our birds: the male capercaillie is about the size of a large turkey, measuring almost a metre long and weighing as much as 4 kilograms. The slightly smaller black grouse is still an impressive bird, though it is much lighter than his cousin, at about 1.2 kilograms. During their unusual courtship behaviour, up to a dozen rival males gather at dawn at a site that has been in use for decades, perhaps centuries, for this ritual. There they will spend several hours posturing, holding court and generally showing off. Occasionally these stand-offs will end in a flurry of claws and feathers with a brief bout of actual fighting, although more often than not the rival birds simply square up to one another like young men at a nightclub, constantly threatening each other, but never actually coming to blows.

The leks of both the black grouse and the capercaillie are fascinating to watch, especially as the posturing and movement is accompanied by a series of bizarre sounds: the black grouse makes a noise rather like the cooing of doves; while the capercaillie's call is remarkably reminiscent of a champagne cork popping and the liquid being poured, but in reverse – so starting with the liquid gurgle and ending with the 'pop'!

All this effort is directed at the non-performers: the watching females, who stand at a discreet distance around the edge of the lek. They may seem passive, but it is they who will choose the dominant male. The winning male gets the lion's share of the spoils, often mating with all the females while his rivals fail to breed at all. So although the lek may look rather comical, its purpose is deadly serious.

Lekking occurs among a diverse range of birds and other animals around the world, including several species of gamebird, hummingbirds, waders, fruit bats and even walruses. It happens when there is no need to defend a territory, because food is widely spread and available at that time. This also means that once the male has mated with the female he has nothing further to do with the raising of its young.

OPPOSITE: Black grouse have an extraordinary and spectacular courtship display in winter in which males square up to one another in a performance known as a 'lek'.

FOLLOWING PAGES: Grey herons are amongst our earliest breeding birds, building their huge nests in the branches of trees, using twigs.

Boxing hares

There can be few more classic signs of the end of winter and the onset of spring than the display of brown hares 'boxing'. It is an extraordinary sight to behold, especially as it appears to be completely spontaneous behaviour. At one moment a group of hares seem to be sitting quietly in a field, contentedly feeding or watching for danger, then, in an instant, one will begin to chase another, but after running a few feet will stop, turn around and stand bolt upright. It is then that they will begin to 'box' one another like prizefighters. The two will usually come to blows for just a few seconds, before one turns tail and flees. This behaviour has earned them the name 'Mad March hare', as popularised in Lewis Carroll's celebrated *Alice's Adventures in Wonderland.*

For a long time it was assumed that these were two rival males, fighting to have the right to mate with the observing females, in the same way that red deer stags take part in the annual rut, or male black grouse perform their 'lek'. In fact the two participants are not rivals, but potential mates. The chasing hare is the male, and the other the female.

She boxes him to test his mettle; only after a number of bouts, when she feels sure he is tough enough to provide the right genes for her precious offspring, will she finally succumb and allow him to mate with her. If she does choose to run, he may struggle to catch up with her; after all, hares are the fastest land mammal in Britain, reaching speeds of up to 45 miles per hour, or almost twice as fast as Usain Bolt!

Hares' incredible turn of speed may have evolved because, unlike rabbits, they do not dig burrows, and so they do not have an underground escape route from predators. Instead they either run, or make shallow scrapes in the ground known as 'forms', where they crouch flat, folding their long ears back and staying stock still so that they cannot be seen.

The hare's ability to run very fast and then apparently vanish into thin air meant that humans attributed magical qualities to these animals, including a strong link with springtime fertility (hares also give birth to their first brood of young, known as 'leverets', in early spring). These beliefs were so prevalent in our pagan culture that when Christianity arrived on these islands, almost two millennia ago, to ensure our adoption of the Christian calendar the hare was adopted as the symbol of Easter. So the 'Easter bunny' that we all know and love is in fact not a rabbit at all, but a hare!

Boxing hares are one of the signs that spring is just around the corner. This rite of passage allows the female to assess a potential suitor by challenging him to a fight as he approaches her.

HARES AND LEVERETS

Hares can have between two and four litters of young each year, which are usually born between February and September. While they are very young, these leverets are greatly at risk from predators, in particular rooks and crows, as well as badgers and foxes.

Unlike rabbits, hares do not burrow under ground and so live their life in relatively open spaces such as farmland and fields, which exposes them to greater danger from predators. As a result, these mammals have evolved to run at great speed to evade capture, but another way by which they try to escape detection is by creating scrapes called 'forms' in the ground in areas of long grass. They protect themselves by lying absolutely still on the ground, tucked into their form with their ears pressed flat along their backs. The hare will remain like this until the very last minute that it is discovered, as its best defence is in staying still and camouflaged. Brown hares venture out during the day but are also active at night, when the darkness offers them better protection against predators. In the dark, predators must rely on their sense of smell to detect them, but nature has also devised a way of protecting them here too, as leverets are born without a scent, making them hard to find for a few weeks until it develops and the leveret has grown.

Adders arrive

Like all our native and introduced species of reptile, adders hibernate during the winter when it would be impossible for them to find enough food to survive. But even so, adders are pretty tough and hardy, living further north than any of the world's 3,400 or so different species of snake, with a habitat that reaches just inside the Arctic Circle. After a long hibernation, on mild late-winter days, when the sun shines and the temperature begins to rise, these snakes emerge from their hiding places and bask in the weak sunshine in an attempt to warm up.

Most emerging adders appear on the heaths of southern England – Dorset, Hampshire and Surrey – where sandy soils on the edges of woodland, their favourite habitat, heat up more quickly than in other areas. Early mornings often see these attractive snakes basking in the sunshine on south-facing slopes.

The adder is well known as Britain's only venomous snake. Their dark skin, with its distinctive zigzag markings, is not only a good way to identify them but also helps them warm up more quickly than if they were a lighter shade. Like all reptiles, adders are cold-blooded, which means they need to raise their body temperature through an external heat source such as the sun before they can become active.

After a long hibernation, when the sun shines and the temperature starts to rise, these snakes emerge from their hiding place and bask in the weak sunshine.

At this time of year adders may be seen doing what looks like a dance, as two snakes entwine their bodies around each other. This was once thought to be a courtship display prior to mating, but we now know that it is usually an act performed by male adders who are trying to drive others out of their territory.

By mid-to-late morning, if the sun continues to shine and temperatures heat up, the adders will quietly slip away from these exposed places and go off to hunt and feed – mainly on small rodents such as voles and mice, but also taking frogs, newts and, later in the season, the eggs of ground-nesting birds.

As with other hibernating creatures, emerging this soon in the season is a calculated risk. If the fine weather continues, those that come out early will have the advantage over their tardier cousins; but if frosts and snow appear, as they may well do in March, they will struggle to find enough food to survive.

The adder is the toughest of all Britain's reptiles, and these venomous snakes often emerge long before the end of winter.

Our unpredictable winters

When reminiscing about their childhood, older people can often be heard remembering the times when 'we used to have proper winters', with plenty of snow and ice. But is this just nostalgia, or are they remembering it right? Are today's winters really milder than they used to be – and if they are, what effect might this be having on our wildlife?

The answer to the first question is 'up to a point'! Britain has seen some cold winters in the past few years – notably the winter of 2009–10, which was the fourth coldest overall since the Second World War, and in some parts of Britain colder than any winter since the infamous 'Big Freeze' of 1962–63. But in recent decades the trend has certainly been towards milder winters, with a long run without a really cold winter from the mid-1980s into the opening decade of the twenty-first century. Average temperatures during these years were often several degrees higher than the long-term average, with very little snow or even frost, especially in southern and western Britain, where the climate is milder than the north and east in any case.

Whether or not this is caused by global climate change is a controversial issue, as the effect on weather patterns in a particular year and in a specific area is very hard to predict. However, if the current trend does become a more permanent pattern it is likely to have a considerable effect on our wildlife.

There are two areas to consider: short-term and long-term effects. In the short-term, mild spells in winter can play havoc with what we often call 'nature's calendar'. Hibernating mammals such as the hedgehog may emerge during a spell of warm weather in the middle of winter, but as soon as the weather turns, and they are unable to find food, they are in trouble. Although they may attempt to hibernate again, if their body weight is below a critical level they will not have enough energy left to make it through to the spring. Insects such as bumblebees and butterflies may also emerge on warm, sunny days; but unlike hedgehogs they are able to retreat into their winter hideaways if the weather turns cold again.

Mild winters are good news for parasites and diseases, which are often killed off by a cold snap, but this can have a negative effect on all sorts of creatures, including mammals and birds.

In really mild winters, flowers bloom, leaves unfurl and birds begin nesting as early as January – sometimes even before Christmas. This may seem suicidal, but for birds that normally have several broods in a single season, such as blackbirds and song thrushes, it can make sense. If the weather holds, and they are able to find enough food for their chicks, they may be able to get a clutch of

Britain has seen some cold winters in the past few years ... But in recent decades the trend has certainly been towards milder winters.

OPPOSITE TOP: A small garden bumblebee sits frozen on a twig, covered with a layer of ice crystals.

OPPOSITE BOTTOM: Two seven-spot ladybirds perch on a wire during a hard winter frost.

eggs laid, incubated and hatched, and a family of youngsters out of the nest and fending for themselves before winter returns. More often, however, a cold snap, with snow and ice making it impossible to find enough food, puts paid to their chances pretty rapidly.

Other birds have changed their migratory habits in milder winters, too, choosing to spend the season here in Britain instead of heading south to warmer locations. Chiffchaffs and blackcaps are both relatively short-distance travellers, so they usually spend the winter in Spain, Portugal or North Africa rather than heading across the Equator. Chiffchaffs have always overwintered in small numbers in the southwest of England, and a run of mild winters led to a rise in numbers doing so. They are usually found settled near water where there are plenty of small insects on which they can feed.

The blackcap's story is more complicated, though. In recent years, sightings of blackcaps have been reported more and more in town and city gardens during our mild winter months, mostly feeding on bird tables. It was naturally assumed that these were native birds which had decided not to migrate south for the winter, but in fact these blackcaps had come from Germany and Austria, having flown in the 'wrong' direction (westwards as opposed to southwest) the previous autumn.

The climate and the handouts from generous humans who feed garden birds enabled the blackcap to survive the British winter; they would then fly back to their breeding grounds earlier than birds that had overwintered in Spain or North Africa, and because they returned early they grabbed all the best territories. Incredibly, within a couple of decades the entire population of blackcaps have changed their behaviour, and they all now spend the winter here in Britain.

These continental blackcaps begin to depart our shores in late February, about the time when the first long-distance migrants are beginning to return to Britain. These early arrivals include the sand martin, wheatear and the occasional swallow, but this is a risky strategy: these early birds may bag the best territory, but a late cold snap in March can mean there are no insects to eat, and so they will perish.

In the longer term, these runs of mild winters will allow small birds to increase their populations, as far fewer die of starvation than during cold winters, but small mammals may benefit from a snowy winter, as they are able to hide from predators beneath the layer of snow.

The blackcap has taken advantage of a run of mild winters and our habit of feeding garden birds, and can now be seen in winter as well as spring and summer.

But both birds and mammals – along with us humans – eagerly await the final melting of the winter's snow, and the signs that, little by little, spring is about to begin.

SPRING
INTO
SUMMER

Spring explodes in a frantic frenzy of activity, as millions of wild creatures settle down to breed and raise a family, insects emerge and wild flowers begin to bloom. At this time of year Britain becomes a global crossroads, as millions of migrant birds return home from their African winter quarters, while others leave us, heading north to breed in the High Arctic. Trees are coming into leaf, birdsong fills the air, and around our coasts the seas burst with incredible marine life: from seahorses to sharks and whelks to whales. This is just the start of the busiest period of the year, which culminates on midsummer's day, the true start of summer.

THREE MONTHS AFTER our journey through the annual cycle of Britain's wildlife began, in the dead of winter, what has changed? The land is still gripped by the chill winds of March; frosts trouble gardeners and wildlife alike; and from time to time the ground may be carpeted with a light covering of late-winter snow.

But we are about to embark on what must surely be the most exciting season in nature's varied calendar: spring. Towards the end of March – the day of the spring equinox, when every place on the planet experiences a roughly equal balance of 12 hours of daylight and 12 hours of darkness – spring will officially begin. Nature's rollercoaster has inched its way up the slope to the summit, and now begins to rapidly speed up as it dives into the new season. Over the next three months, until we reach the summer solstice at around the end of June, the days will continue to lengthen, the temperatures will rise, and a great explosion of activity will take place.

The 'race to reproduce' – the essential process of passing on genetic heritage from one generation to the next – peaks during the months of April, May and June, as birds, mammals, insects, reptiles, amphibians, plants and many other organisms enter their breeding season. They lay their eggs, raise their young, and do everything in their power to ensure their offspring's survival; because many species may never get another chance to breed in their brief but eventful lives.

The switch from winter to spring is not an event but a process. Since the winter solstice, just before Christmas, the hours of daylight have gradually increased, day after day and week after week. This is fixed; but the change in temperatures from cold to heat is not. Winters may be mild or icy; springs early or late; the weather wet or dry, and these factors vary not only from year to year but also depending on where in the country you are.

Light and warmth are the key factors that enable plants and animals to reproduce. They allow plants to begin the process of growth that will eventually result in buds, flowers and seeds, and creatures of every size and shape to find food and produce energy – essential parts of the process of reproduction. This applies, of course, to the majority of creatures that spend the whole of their lives

in this country; but also equally to those that travel to Britain from other parts of the world to spend the spring and summer months here in order to take advantage of our long hours of daylight and plentiful supplies of food in these months.

Throughout the next month or so the return of migratory birds from Africa gets underway: the greatest wildlife phenomenon on the face of the planet, it involves hundreds of millions of birds. But equally incredible are the unseen migrations; those of millions, perhaps billions, of insects such as butterflies and moths; and the global journeys of marine creatures, which arrive off our shores during this period too.

Early spring is also a time for departures. The ducks, geese and swans that have spent the winter months on our estuaries, marshes and reservoirs head north to breed in the High Arctic. Other birds, including waders such as the turnstone, sanderling and knot, are also heading north, and pass through Britain on their journey from Africa to the Arctic Circle. Having stopped here to feed, they continue on their way.

For many resident creatures, including small mammals, birds, amphibians and some insects, activity is already well underway even as the spring equinox arrives. Virtually all our resident songbirds, such as thrushes, robins, finches and tits, are now singing – some have been doing so since the turn of the New Year (see page 57) – while frogs and newts have laid their spawn and voles and mice are already raising their first of many litters. Foxes and badgers are giving birth, and soon their cubs will emerge from the earth or sett to explore the wider world for the first time.

One of the key factors influencing success or failure during the coming breeding season is the weather. A late cold snap, bringing severe frosts, below-zero temperatures and even snow, can have a very serious effect on a wide range of plants and animals, including early blooming wild flowers, breeding birds and emerging insects.

But as well as the weather, which may change from year to year and even week to week during the early part of spring, there is also the vexed question of climate change. Vexed because, although we are able to measure and even

predict overall changes to the global climate, our local weather is so variable that it can be very difficult to judge long-term trends amidst the swings between cold late springs and warm early ones.

What we do know is that while some creatures have shown an extraordinary ability to adapt to the effects of climate change, such as the trend towards earlier springs over the past few decades, others are far less able to do so. Birds that have several broods of chicks each year, such as the blackbird and song thrush, can take a gamble and nest earlier than single-brooded species such as the blue tit. Even if their first attempt fails, these multi-brooded birds can try again; whereas if a pair of blue tits gambles all and fails, it will not have another chance until the following year – by which time these short-lived little birds may no longer be with us.

Migrant birds are also far less able to adapt than resident birds: the tiny changes in day length are what trigger their return to our shores, meaning that if spring has already come and gone by the time they arrive, there may be nothing on which to feed their hungry young.

Even if birds and other wild creatures do succeed in raising a family, their troubles may not be over. Wet summers and droughts cause different problems for different species, but a more extreme climate, with a greater proportion of extreme weather events, is never good news for our wildlife.

By late June, the majority of birds and mammals, and many insects and plants too, have either succeeded or failed in the annual act of reproduction. This is now a less frenzied period: with plenty of food and long hours of daylight in which to find it. Birds use this time to moult their tatty plumage into fresh new feathers, to prepare for the coming autumn and winter, while mammals spend much of the time simply loafing around, as food is plentiful. The season that follows – the summer – is the peak time for many wild flowers and the insects that feed on them; for them, their moment in the sun is yet to come.

THIS PAGE: A one-week-old fawn
finds his feet and takes his first steps.

OPPOSITE: Baby squirrels stay
in the safety of their nests until
they are about ten weeks old.

Bluebells in bloom

The sudden changes of weather in spring, as March winds give way to April showers, are vital to all wildlife, since rain and sunshine are the ingredients that plants and animals need in order to thrive at this crucial time of year. But for wild flowers these elements are even more essential, and throughout Britain one particular flower sums up this time of year: the bluebell.

The bluebell regularly tops any poll for Britain's favourite wild flower. This may be because each individual plant is very attractive, with tall stalks and drooping mauve flower heads, but it is also undoubtedly because of the magnificent displays they make when thousands bloom en masse in our woodlands and forests, confirming the fact that spring has well and truly arrived.

Unlike other iconic British plants and animals – the cowslip or buttercup, the robin or the red squirrel – the bluebell also has the advantage of rarity. They may be a commonplace sight across much of this country, but globally these flowers are fairly scarce, with a quite-restricted range in those countries that border Europe's Atlantic seaboard: north-west Spain, France, the Low Countries, Ireland and of course Britain. Indeed, our damp, mild climate supports more than half the total world population of this iconic flower. Bluebells are perennial plants, growing from a bulb that is able to store energy during the autumn and winter months to produce the flowers each spring. Each bulb produces up to six long, green leaves, and a single stem on which the individual flowers cluster. Their characteristic sweet scent creates a delightful atmosphere in spring woodlands. The flowers are nectar-rich, so they are welcomed by early insects including their main pollinator: the bumblebee.

Bluebells are a classic indicator species of ancient woodland, found from Devon and Cornwall in the southwest, through central England, East Anglia and northern England, to the very north of Scotland. Indeed, they are only absent from the island groups of the far north and west: Lewis, Harris, Orkney and Shetland.

Famous bluebell woods include Chawton Park Woods in Hampshire, close to Jane Austen's childhood home, Ebbor Gorge, near Wells in Somerset, Pencelli Forest in southwest Wales, Castle Eden Dene in County Durham, and Glasdrum Wood in Argyll and Bute. The timing of the displays varies from south to north (from early April through to mid-May), and depends on the prevailing weather conditions in any particular spring.

This well-known and well-loved wild flower has attracted a wide range of folk-names, including fairy bells, bellflower, wild hyacinth, fairy thimble and

Bluebells are one of our best-loved wild flowers, forming a carpet of colour on our forest floors in April and May.

blue bottle. And like many of our native plants, bluebells are not just attractive but useful too. They have long been employed in folk medicine as diuretics, and they may prove to have wider uses as cures for diseases.

In recent years, Britain's bluebells have come under threat from hybridisation with a non-native species, the Spanish bluebell. Closely related to our native bluebell, this is a popular garden flower that has inevitably escaped the boundaries of our gardens and spread into wild habitats, where it then crossbreeds with the indigenous bluebells. The Spanish and hybrid varieties have taller, straighter stems, and the flowers do not droop as those of the native variety do. They also have a less powerful scent.

Once the month of May is out, most of Britain's bluebells have gone over, setting their small black seeds on the forest floor, ready to create a new generation of flowers the following spring.

Conservationists are working to remove these invaders from our woodlands; and like other wild flowers, bluebells are also protected by laws against uprooting them – though sadly people are still occasionally tempted to take them from the wild for use in their own gardens.

Once the month of May is out, most of Britain's bluebells have gone over, setting their small black seeds on the forest floor, ready to create a new generation of flowers the following spring.

Bumblebees flitting from flower to flower in search of nectar are one of the first signs that spring may finally be here.

A buzz in the air

On sunny spring days you may be surprised to see the movement of an insect as it patrols the borders of a garden or a woodland edge. But although temperatures are still fairly low at this point in the year, there is just enough warmth in the air to allow an early queen bumblebee to emerge from her winter hideaway and search for precious, energy-giving nectar. In turn, she and all the insects that follow her will help to spread the flowers' pollen, performing a vital service in return for food.

   She is able to emerge so early in the season partly due to her relatively large size, because smaller creatures lose heat much more rapidly than larger ones,

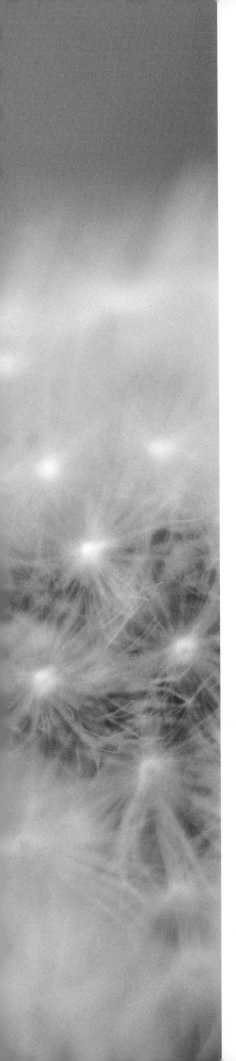

due to the higher ratio of their surface area to their internal volume. This means that once this bulky insect has managed to warm up, she can take to the air.

The earliest queens to emerge are usually those of the buff-tailed bumblebee – often known by its scientific name *Bombus terrestris* – which may appear as early as January or February, but are usually first seen in mid-March. The queens are considerably larger than the workers and males, averaging 15–17 millimetres in length compared with 10–14 millimetres for the others.

Other early species include the white-tailed bumblebee (*Bombus lucorum*) and the aptly named early bumblebee (*Bombus pratorum*). Queens will cruise around early blooming flowers such as crocuses or primroses, and then alight on their flowers to feed on their nectar.

Once the queen has built up her energy reserves she will then make a zigzag flight low to the ground, a sign that she is looking for the ideal place to make her nest. She must work very hard in order to get into breeding condition – it has been estimated that she will need to visit more than 5,000 flowers every single day – or roughly eight blooms a minute – in order to do so.

It has always been known that bees play a vital role in pollinating both wild flowers and crops of fruit and vegetables, but recent studies have revealed that the importance of wild insects such as bumblebees and solitary bees is far greater than once thought. It had been assumed that honeybees carry out up to 90 per cent of insect pollination, but with the dramatic declines in their population in recent years, wild bees have taken on a far greater importance. For the UK alone, insect pollination of commercial crops is valued at about £400 million per year.

Not all flowers and crops are pollinated by insects: wind is also a very important factor in this process, especially for catkins and early blooming flowers. The dandelion is known to generations of children for its 'clocks', used in childhood games; these are of course the seed heads, each of which contains up to 2,000 separate seeds that will be carried on the breeze, travelling distances of up to 500 metres away from the parent plant.

Dandelions are not the first spring flowers – that honour goes to snowdrops, crocuses and primroses – but as spring progresses they soon appear on lawns, grassy areas and fields. First to appear are the characteristic leaves, the shape of which gives the flower its name (from the French *dent de lion*, meaning 'lion's tooth'); then the custard-yellow flowers, and finally the famous 'clocks'. By this time spring is well underway and the process of pollination is helping to set plants up for the next phase of their lifecycle.

A ladybird perched on an early dandelion 'clock' is another sign that spring is well and truly underway.

The migrants' return

Bird migration has long been one of the natural world's greatest mysteries, and although we now have a greater scientific understanding both of the reasons behind and the mechanics of these epic journeys, it remains the most awe-inspiring and impressive of all natural events.

To many people, it may seem bizarre that a bird should choose to leave the familiar place where it was born and raised and risk travelling such a long way in order to spend the winter elsewhere. Yet as scientists have long pointed out, the risks of staying put for the winter may be at least as great, if not greater, than migrating. The key issue is food: if a bird is unable to find enough food to survive, it has no choice but to travel to a place where food is more plentiful and reliable. And by spending half the year in Africa and the other half here in Britain, the bird gets the best of both worlds: the optimum place to spend the winter which is warm and welcoming; and plenty of food and long hours in which to find it during the northern summer.

It would seem logical that the weather plays a part in the timing of these birds' return to our shores; and indeed, towards the end of their journey it sometimes does, when they may be held up by northerly winds keeping them on the other side of the English Channel, or they may arrive here a few days early because high pressure and fine weather has enabled faster travel.

But the driving force behind the timing of migration is not weather, nor is it the rise in air temperatures that happens in spring; in fact, it is light. Each bird has the ability to detect tiny changes in day length around the time of the spring equinox. These trigger chemical changes in their brain that impel them to set off on the long and arduous journey north – a journey that may be as much as 9,600 kilometres (6,000 miles) for birds wintering near the southern tip of Africa.

The timing of migration does, however, vary considerably between different species. The first arrivals reach us in March, and include a small wader – the little ringed plover, which nests on the shingle banks of rivers and in gravel-pits; the garganey – our only summering species of duck, also known as the 'summer teal'; and songbirds such as the wheatear and sand martin.

Wheatears (the name derives from an Anglo-Saxon phrase meaning 'white arse', because of the bird's white rump) may appear on beaches in southern England, and can be easily identified by their sandy-coloured plumage and upright stance. Sand martins, the smallest member of the swallow family in Britain, often gather over large bodies of water such as reservoirs, where they

The knot is a passage migrant, passing through Britain in spring on its way north to breed in the High Arctic.

swoop low over the surface to pick up the first tiny insects of the season. They can be told apart from the more familiar swallow and house martin by their colour: sand martins are brown above and white below, with a brown band across the breast.

Arriving so early can give them a huge advantage over other birds, as it enables them to pick the best nesting sites and get off to a flying start. But if they get things wrong, and arrive here during a spell of cold, wet weather, they may well starve to death because of the lack of insects – allowing the latecomers to triumph.

Although these few species of migrant songbirds do reach Britain during March, the period between the beginning of April and early May sees the arrival of the bulk of them. During just a few weeks, well over ten million individuals of more than 20 different species reach our shores: including warblers, flycatchers, chats, swallows, martins, swifts and cuckoos.

Exactly when the main arrival takes place varies – much like Easter, it can happen at any time from late March through to late April. This depends mostly on the prevailing weather conditions both in Britain and especially immediately to the south of here, on the other side of the English Channel. Low-pressure weather systems, bringing persistent rain and cold northerly winds, usually block migrants; while high pressure, with clear skies and fine, sunny weather, encourages them to make that final crossing of the water to reach Britain.

Most songbirds migrate by night: the cooler air enables them to fly faster and more efficiently, while it is also the best way to avoid day-flying predators such as birds of prey. The exceptions are the swallows, martins and swifts, which must feed on flying insects as they travel (instead of building up fat reserves before they leave, as do the other migrant songbirds) and so migrate by day. Once dawn approaches, night migrants will look for a suitable place to rest and feed to build up their energy for the next leg of their journey.

This is why south coast headlands and offshore islands, such as Dungeness in Kent, Portland in Dorset, and the Isles of Scilly, see such concentrations of migrants on spring mornings, and why these places have traditionally attracted birdwatchers and been the sites of bird observatories. Bad weather brings an even greater bonanza: in fine conditions many small birds will simply continue overhead until they are well inland; but during rain and storms they will make landfall as soon as they can.

Early-to-mid April brings the main arrival: swallows and house martins, and the warblers: whitethroat and lesser whitethroat to hedgerows, reed and sedge warblers to wetlands, and garden, wood and willow warblers to woodlands and forests. Two birds of the western oak woodlands, pied flycatcher and redstart, also arrive from mid-April, as does the cuckoo. Some birds stop as soon as they

During just a few weeks, well over ten million individuals of more than twenty different species reach our shores.

As their name suggests, sand martins build their nest by excavating a hole in a sandy bank – often on the edge of a river where there is plenty of insect food for their hungry young.

reach southern Britain; many others carry on, either to breed in Scotland or even across the North Sea to Scandinavia.

Later in April, the first swifts arrive – these extraordinary birds have flown all the way from Britain to Africa and back without ever touching down, as they are able to feed and even sleep on the wing. Parties of swifts, uttering their ear-piercing, high-pitched screaming calls, are a classic sight and sound across Britain's city skylines, as the swift has adapted to live as an urban bird. Once nesting in crevices in cliffs and crags, swifts now mainly nest in tall buildings, catching tiny insects in the air above our urban jungles.

Some migrants rarely arrive before May. These include a declining songbird, the spotted flycatcher – whose upright stance and technique of flying off a perch to grab a passing insect makes it easy to identify – and an even scarcer migrant, the turtle dove. The turtle dove's population is dropping so rapidly, because of habitat loss at home and persecution by hunters on its migration routes through the Mediterranean, that it may well disappear as a British breeding bird in the next few decades.

Two other groups of birds quicken the pulse of birdwatchers at this time of year. Several species, known as 'passage migrants', pass through Britain in spring, on the way north to breed in Scandinavia, Iceland and the Arctic. These include waders such as the whimbrel (a smaller version of the curlew, which breeds in small numbers on Shetland), and the tortoiseshell-coloured turnstone; and the little gull and black tern, the former the world's smallest gull and the latter one of Europe's three species of 'marsh tern'.

There may also be birds that do not belong here at all: rare southern vagrants that have either continued their migration north farther than they intended (a process known as 'spring overshooting', which happens when a large area of high pressure over Europe brings light southerly winds), or those from farther east which have drifted across the North Sea on easterly winds as they head back to their breeding grounds. The former include exotic birds such as the comical-looking hoopoe and the bizarrely colourful bee-eater, both of which mostly nest in southern Europe but occasionally breed here once they have arrived. Sightings of the bee-eater in particular are a relatively rare thing in Britain, though, varying between 14 and 132 birds each year, but since 2002 there have been two recorded occasions of the birds breeding in this country. The latter grouping of visiting birds includes the bluethroat, a closer relative of the nightingale, which looks rather like a robin, but with a bright blue breast instead of a red one! Bluethroats, along with other eastern visitors, breed in Scandinavia and eastern Europe.

The bee-eater may look like it belongs in the tropics, but this exotic bird now nests just across the English Channel, and could possibly colonise southern Britain in the next few years.

The call of the cuckoo

Apart perhaps from the swallow, no other migratory bird is so associated with the arrival of spring as the cuckoo. For centuries, in the middle of April 'cuckoo fairs' were held up and down the country to welcome this bird back from its wintering grounds in Africa and to mark what they hoped was also the arrival of spring and warmer weather.

The cuckoo's special place in our history and heritage is not because of its appearance; a shy creature, it is rarely seen out in the open for very long. Instead the bird's fame rests on two things: its extraordinary call and its habit – unique amongst British birds – of always laying its eggs in other birds' nests.

This habit – known to ornithologists as 'brood parasitism' – is rare in nature: out of more than 220 bird families in the world, just six have evolved this breeding behaviour, including the majority of the cuckoos that are found in the Old World.

Once a female cuckoo has mated with the male, she flies around an area looking for suitable nests of her preferred host. In Britain, the vast majority of cuckoos usually lay their eggs in the nest of one of just three species: the meadow pipit, dunnock or reed warbler. Whether these are easier to dupe than other species we are not sure; but the partnership is a long-established one. Cuckoos always lay in the nest of the same species that raised them, so they are able to identify the host and seek out their nest. They have also evolved the extraordinary ability to change the colour and pattern of their eggs so they mimic those of the host.

With their pointed wings and long tail, in flight a cuckoo looks rather like a falcon or sparrowhawk. This is probably no coincidence: their resemblance to a low-flying bird of prey may well have evolved to provoke small birds into flying off their nest to attack the intruder into their territory. By doing so, this then allows the female to fly down to the unguarded nest and rapidly lay her single egg. If the nest already has a clutch of eggs she will usually remove one and drop it onto the ground or into the water below, thereby fooling the host into thinking that nothing has changed.

It may seem bizarre that any bird should choose to lay its egg in another bird's nest, and therefore forgo its parental duties, yet when you think about it, this strategy makes perfect evolutionary sense. Feeding a hungry brood of youngsters is time-consuming and uses a lot of energy, so by fooling the foster

This enormous cuckoo chick, barely managing to stay in the reed warbler's nest, dwarfs its host parent.

parents from the host species into doing all the hard work, the female cuckoo is able to lay far more eggs: up to 20 in a single season, compared with perhaps four to six eggs if she had to raise the chicks herself.

By putting each of these eggs into a different nest, she is also maximising the chances of raising lots of young; compared with 'normal' species of bird in which a single attack by a predator can destroy a whole clutch of eggs or a nest full of chicks, and thereby end that season's breeding attempt.

Cuckoo eggs hatch earlier than those of their host species, which enables the newborn chick to indulge in some extraordinary behaviour. Soon after it is born, the baby cuckoo will eject all of the host eggs from the nest, arching its back and pressing its wings and feet against the sides to lift the egg over the rim.

Even more bizarrely, the host parents immediately accept this huge chick as their own, feeding it during every daylight hour. It gets bigger and bigger, ultimately filling the whole of the nest, by which time it is considerably larger than its foster parents. Eventually it fledges and leaves the nest, and even more incredibly, it then flies all the way to Africa – a journey of several thousand miles – without ever meeting its true parents.

You might think, then, that cuckoos should be doing rather well in Britain; after all, they ought to be able to produce far more young in a single year than any other breeding birds. Yet the truth is that during the past few decades the numbers of cuckoo have declined faster than those of almost any other British bird – by two-thirds since 1980.

The baby cuckoo will eject all of the host eggs from the nest, arching its back and pressing its wings and feet against the sides to lift the egg over the rim.

This is likely to be the result of environmental problems both at home and abroad. Here in Britain the number of the larger caterpillars the cuckoo feeds on has been declining dramatically because of the widespread use of agricultural insecticides and loss of hedgerow habitat; while in Africa a combination of habitat loss and climate change (the two are often, though not always, related) is affecting both the cuckoo's wintering grounds and also the vital stopover locations it needs on its migratory journey.

Barn owl chicks may look cute, but if there is a shortage of food the larger one may kill and eat its smaller sibling to avoid starving to death.

Survival of the fittest

As we saw in the winter months, the barn owl is very vulnerable to bad weather, especially prolonged spells of rain, which can quickly make its feathers waterlogged so that it is unable to hunt. So for barn owls, the period between late spring and high summer is a crucial one; if the weather is fine this is when they may make good the losses of earlier in the year by raising a family.

Unlike most other birds, which usually lay a full clutch of eggs before they begin to incubate (thus ensuring that the chicks all hatch at the same time), barn owls have a very different strategy. The female will begin to incubate as soon as the first of up to six eggs is laid. She will then lay another egg every two or three

Barn owls hunt mainly at dawn, dusk and through the night, when they float low across the ground, listening for the tiny rustles that reveal the presence of their prey.

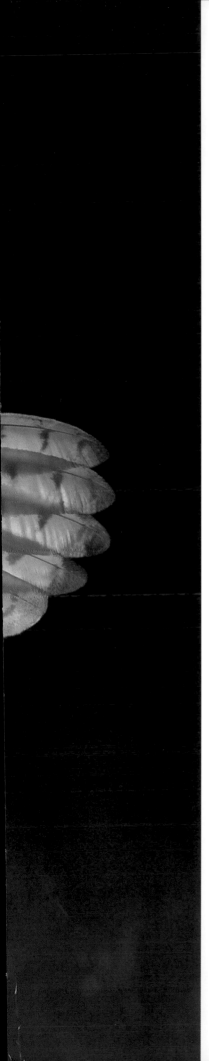

days until the clutch is complete, which means that the eldest chick hatches out as much as two weeks earlier than the youngest.

This strategy has evolved to maximise the number of young raised each year. This is because the availability of the barn owl's favourite food – voles and mice – is unpredictable and cyclical, so that in some years there may be a glut of these little animals, and in other years a shortage. By having a family of different-sized young, the barn owl ensures that in a good year, when voles are plentiful, all of its offspring will survive. In a bad year – when these rodents are in short supply, perhaps combined with a wet summer which makes hunting them much harder – only the eldest and strongest of their young will survive.

In a bizarre and gruesome twist to this breeding strategy, when food is really scarce the older and stronger siblings will often kill and eat the younger, weaker ones in a rare example of cannibalism amongst birds.

Barn owls hunt mainly at dawn, dusk and through the night, when they are able to float low across the ground, listening for the tiny rustles that reveal the presence of their prey. They have three special adaptations to enable them to do so: first, the very soft flight feathers that make virtually no sound; second, asymmetric ears, with one higher than the other, which enable them to work out the exact position of their victim; and finally, a heart-shaped face, which magnifies and focuses any sound made by the vole towards the barn owl's ears, rather like a man-made parabolic reflector which sound recordists use to amplify distant sounds. Together, these make the barn owl one of the most specialised of all predators.

Barn owl numbers plummeted in the years following the Second World War, first because of a reduction in the number of voles and a loss of habitat as a result of intensive agriculture; and second because pesticides such as DDT affected all birds at the top of the food chain by thinning their eggshells, so that the chicks failed to hatch. Since then, the population has begun to bounce back, helped by the widespread provision of artificial nestboxes in barns and other farm buildings, which encourage barn owls to nest.

Nevertheless these birds still remain vulnerable, not least because their low-flying habits mean they often fall victim to motor vehicles, especially as they hunt along roadside verges where there are plenty of mice and voles in the long grass. Unseasonably wet weather in late spring, when the owls have chicks in the nest, is also affecting barn owls.

The barn owl is the consummate
nocturnal hunter, swooping low over
the ground on its soft, silent wings
in search of unsuspecting voles.

Run, rabbit, run

Although the 'Easter bunny' story almost certainly derives from the rabbit's larger relative the brown hare (see page 67), rabbits are nevertheless closely associated with spring; partly because, like many other mammals, they are less active in winter and because late winter and spring are peak seasons for breeding.

Depending on the severity of the winter, female rabbits give birth any time from February through to August. Litters of between three and seven young (known as 'pups') can be born every five or six weeks throughout this period – hence the phrase 'breeding like rabbits'!

As with most mammals the pups are born helpless, blind and naked; their eyes open after ten days or so, and they stay in the safety of their hole for three and a half weeks before they are ready to leave it. After this they develop very rapidly indeed – if the conditions are right (good weather and plenty of available food), a rabbit is able to breed at just four months old. Their astonishing fertility makes rabbits the favoured prey of many other creatures, including buzzards, owls, stoats and weasels, and, of course, foxes.

Rabbits are an introduced species, they were brought here by the Normans for food and fur (though some evidence now suggests the Romans may also have brought rabbits to Britain). For centuries the rabbit was quite a scarce animal, carefully guarded in sets of burrows known as warrens, as they represented a valuable source of meat.

Numbers gradually rose as farming practices changed during the nineteenth and twentieth centuries, and by the 1950s the population had reached between 50 and 100 million – comfortably outnumbering the human population of these islands. Then came the devastation wrought by the disease myxomatosis, which led to a slow and painful death for millions of rabbits.

Myxomatosis reduced the UK rabbit population by more than 90 per cent, and left large areas of the countryside virtually rabbit-free. Since then, numbers have risen, and the current population is estimated at just over 40 million. Campaigns to encourage us to eat more rabbit (a cheap, sustainable and healthy form of protein) have so far failed, which is perhaps because of the legacy of myxomatosis but also because of the way in which they are represented to children and adults.

Rabbits continue to provoke very different reactions amongst humans: they are undeniably cute (especially the pups), but they do serious damage to farmland crops and can have negative effects on nature reserves through over-grazing.

Rabbits are sociable animals, living together in underground networks of burrows known as warrens and breeding repeatedly throughout spring and summer.

Rabbits are closely associated with spring; partly because late winter and spring are the peak seasons for breeding.

Modern meadows

The sight – and sound – of a wildflower meadow, an artist's palette of shades and colours, accompanied by the low hum of insects, is one of our most iconic spring and summer wildlife experiences. Great swathes of ox-eye daisies mingle with knapweed, docks and red clover, along with scarce plants such as orchids and oxlips, to create a flower-rich habitat which attracts millions of insects; which in turn provide food for hungry birds.

A pity, then, that there are so few such meadows remaining: more than three million hectares of wildflower meadows (at least 95 per cent, and probably as much as 97 per cent, of the original habitat) have disappeared since the Second World War, leaving less than 100,000 hectares remaining. These lost meadows have been replaced by so-called 'improved' (i.e. heavily fertilised) grassland for hay or silage, or arable crops.

Today, the vast majority of any meadows that remain are on nature reserves, carefully managed by conservationists who follow a strict regime of planting, grazing and mowing that would have come naturally to our ancestors. For them, meadows were the standard method of providing food for their domestic animals throughout the warmer months of the year – as well as a harvest in the late

Wildflower meadows are an increasingly rare sight in the lowland countryside, with more than 98 per cent having disappeared beneath the plough since the Second World War.

summer to produce hay to keep the livestock fed over the winter. This method is considered too inefficient for modern farmers, who instead use high doses of herbicides and pesticides, and specially bred strains of grass, in order to produce a crop as quickly as possible – and indeed several crops over the course of the season.

Where wildflower meadows remain they remind us of how special a habitat they can be. They change throughout the spring and summer seasons, with April and May seeing the first orchids come into bloom – such as the aptly-named early purple, which usually appears at the same time as a more common meadow flower, the cowslip.

> Where wildflower meadows remain they remind us of how special a habitat they can be... As the number of wildflower meadows decline, the more we seem to crave them.

Green-winged, early spider and early marsh orchids also bloom in spring, especially in damper habitats, while rarer flowers include the snake's head fritillary, so-named because its drooping purple flowers, covered with tiny white flecks, resemble a snake's head.

From June onwards a new set of flowers appears: with wonderful names including viper's bugloss, bird's foot trefoil and lady's bedstraw. Many of these are associated with folk remedies – the frothy cream flowers of meadowsweet were scattered across floors to mask less pleasant smells – and the plant was also used as a remedy against malaria.

As the number of wildflower meadows decline, the more we seem to crave them; so much so that in recent years many people have compensated for the lack of these meadows in the wider countryside by creating one of their own in their garden. Once the topsoil is removed to reduce fertility and prevent swamping of selected seeds by established lawn grass, it only takes a single season to create a replica of this lost and much-loved habitat.

Wildflower meadows are not just beautiful but they also provide a range of vital services to the countryside and its ecosystems. By attracting bees, butterflies and other winged insects they facilitate pollination, but they also help lock up carbon dioxide in the soil, encourage biodiversity and, not least, provide a very special place for people to visit and enjoy.

A roe deer seeks refuge in a field of cow parsley. The roe is one of our two native species of deer, the other being the much larger red deer.

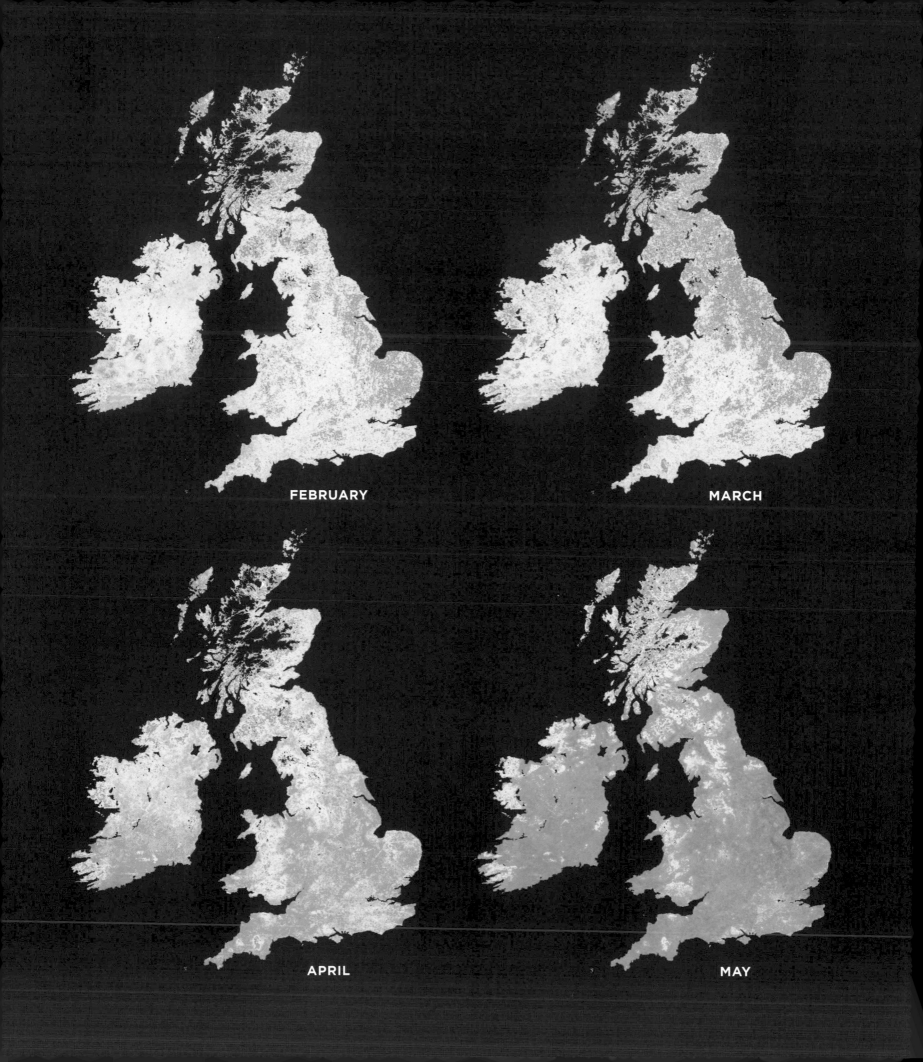

FEBRUARY

MARCH

APRIL

MAY

THE GREENING OF BRITAIN

Over a few months, from February to May, Britain turns green, as plants begin to burst into leaf and bud again (below). The greening of Britain can be measured from space (left), which will inform us how our seasons are shifting year on year. Satellites orbiting above the Earth can record the levels of chlorophyll on our planet (the pigment plants use to photosynthesise) and use this to demonstrate its increase as spring arrives. The false-colour images here show the progression of spring by a measure of chlorophyll concentration, colours changing from cream to brown through yellow to green as the levels increase. The slightly higher levels of chlorophyll in February than in March reflect an unusual pattern that occurred in 2010, when these images were taken. Because that was the coldest winter for 31 years, Britain's vegetation experienced 'winter burn', whereby the intensely cold temperatures combined with other factors to cause the leaves to process water that they could not replace well into March, resulting in brown, desiccated leaves and much-reduced chlorophyll levels until spring truly arrived.

Flight of the butterfly

We usually think of butterflies as summer insects, and indeed most species do emerge from June and through the summer months until August, but several British butterflies have evolved to cope with the cooler weather in spring, and these reach their peak during April and May, fluttering over hedgerows to feed on the nectar from clumps of blossom.

The four main species that regularly overwinter as adults – peacock, comma, brimstone and small tortoiseshell – first appear on sunny days in March and April, and sometimes even February if the weather is especially mild. But the first butterfly to emerge from a chrysalis is usually the orange-tip, whose appearance on warm days from April onwards often coincides with the mass return of our migrant birds, and therefore gives it a special place amongst the symbols of spring. As with other spring butterflies, the orange-tip may appear as early as mid-March, depending on whether or not that particular year's weather has advanced the coming of spring.

Orange-tips are a member of a group of butterfly species known as the 'whites'. Three other species from the same group may also appear at this time: small, large and green-veined whites (collectively lumped under the name 'cabbage white' by the nation's gardeners).

As its name suggests, the male orange-tip is unmistakable, with two bright orange patches on the tips of his forewings. The female orange-tip lacks any orange colour on the wings, so superficially she resembles a small or green-veined white, with white upperwings with black tips and two black spots. However, her underwings have a delicately mottled green pattern which is very different from her relatives.

Orange-tips can be found throughout most of Britain, and frequently they appear in gardens, where they feed on nectar-rich flowers. The female lays her eggs one at a time on two main food plants: garlic mustard and cuckooflower (also known as lady's smock). The reason for keeping a single egg on each plant is that the caterpillars are cannibalistic and will eat one another if they meet!

As well as the orange-tip and the three common and widespread 'whites', several scarcer and more localised butterflies also appear during April. Dingy and grizzled skippers are tiny, drab, easily overlooked butterflies, closely resembling several species of day-flying moth. They are usually found on chalk downlands, flying very low over the surface of the ground where the air is warmer. Dingy skipper, as its name suggests, is a plain brown butterfly with white smudges on the forewings. Its cousin, the grizzled skipper, is more striking, being dark grey, almost black, in colour with a series of white spots around the edges and centre of its wings.

Two other spring butterflies have suffered serious population declines during the past few years, and are now amongst our scarcest species.

Pearl-bordered fritillary is the earliest to appear of the eight species of British fritillary (the name refers to the chequered pattern on the wings), generally being seen from mid-to-late April onwards, and peaking in May. It is one of the smallest fritillaries, with its characteristic black-and-rust coloured upperwings, and a delicately marked combination of silvery white, chestnut brown and buff beneath. Like several species of fritillary, the pearl-bordered fritillary needs a habitat with a mixture of light and shade, and so it thrives in coppiced woodland, where trees are cut to create a dappled pattern of light on the forest floor. Unfortunately, in recent years coppicing has fallen out of favour, and as a result the pearl-bordered fritillary has gone into sharp decline, retreating to its strongholds in the west of England and Scotland, where the damper conditions create the kind of dense woodlands it needs.

The final spring butterfly, the wonderfully named Duke of Burgundy (known to generations of butterfly collectors as 'His Grace'), is the only British representative of a tropical family of butterflies known as the 'metalmarks', because of their bright colours. Superficially similar to a fritillary (and once

PREVIOUS PAGES: Grassland butterflies such as the marbled white have had a tough time in recent years, because of a run of cool, damp summers.

OPPOSITE: The caterpillars of the peacock butterfly feeding on their main food plant, the common stinging nettle.

known as 'Mr Vernon's small fritillary' after a seventeenth-century butterfly collector), this is a tiny butterfly, with a wingspan of just 3 centimetres. It is dark black and speckled with orange above, and paler below, with two lines of silver spots on the lower part of its hind wing.

The Duke of Burgundy is unusual in that it favours two completely different habitats: either chalk or limestone grassland and downland, or sunny clearings in ancient woodland. The species has undergone a severe decline in the past few decades, and in terms of individuals it may now be Britain's rarest butterfly (the large blue has fewer colonies but probably more individuals). One problem for this species has been the increase in numbers of rabbits, which feed on the butterfly's larval food plant, the cowslip.

Fortunately for the Duke of Burgundy, the recent run of dry, sunny springs has enabled it to make a modest comeback, and in some years even to produce a second brood towards the end of the summer. But with climate change and habitat-loss continuing, this may well be the first British butterfly to become extinct here since the large tortoiseshell, which disappeared soon after the end of the Second World War.

On a fine day towards the end of May, the sight of the first spring red admiral, wandering from flower to flower in search of nectar, may not seem to be anything out of the ordinary. But when you discover that this beautiful insect has flown hundreds of miles to get here, all the way from France or even Spain, this sighting becomes rather more remarkable.

Britain's butterflies adopt a range of different lifecycles, including overwintering here as adults, eggs or pupae, but only a few species have evolved the ability to migrate. The red admiral is the commonest and most regular of these, and is one of our most widespread butterflies. Its range extends throughout England, Wales, Ireland and Scotland, including the very northernmost part of the British Isles: the Shetland archipelago, only a few degrees south of the Arctic Circle. Globally this butterfly also has an extensive range, being found throughout North and much of Central America, Europe, Asia and North Africa.

The red admiral is one of our most striking butterflies: with a wingspan of up to 7.5 centimetres, and velvet black upperwings bordered with bands of orange-red and flashes of white. The white flashes, which probably deter predators, are easily visible when the butterfly is in flight.

The name 'admiral' was coined in the early seventeenth century by the pioneering entomologist James Petiver, perhaps because of its grand

The common blue is, as its name suggests, the commonest and most widespread of Britain's eight species of blue butterfly.

appearance; it was later changed to 'admirable', but reverted to 'admiral' in the nineteenth century. In recent years a few red admirals have begun to overwinter as adults in Britain, which means that occasionally they may be seen far earlier in the year than usual (see page 22).

These and the early arriving migrants lay their eggs on nettles, ensuring that fresh generations of their offspring are on the wing throughout summer and autumn. They can often be seen feeding on rotting fruit in autumn, even into November if the weather is fine; though some do migrate to continental Europe.

While red admirals are fairly predictable in their numbers, their close relative the painted lady is certainly not. A little smaller than its cousin, with a paler, more orange coloration, this attractive butterfly is extremely scarce in some years, and very common in others. It too migrates here in May: either from Spain or North Africa, after which the females lay their eggs on thistles. These hatch into caterpillars, which then pupate and finally emerge as adults throughout July and August.

Every now and then we experience a true invasion of this long-distance traveller: the most extraordinary of which occurred in 2009 when tens, perhaps hundreds of millions of painted ladies arrived from late May onwards. They eventually covered the whole of Britain and became by far the commonest butterfly that memorable summer. In the autumn, some were seen leaving our shores, presumably on their way to their home around the Mediterranean.

Other kinds of butterfly, as well as several moths, are also migrants. Clouded yellow butterflies – which superficially resemble the more familiar brimstone but are a more custard-yellow shade with black markings on the wingtips – also have good and bad years; while migrant moths such as the silver y (so-named because of the distinctive y-shaped markings on its closed wings) are more regular and widespread.

Sightings of one day-flying moth may cause both confusion and excitement. As its name suggests, the hummingbird hawkmoth closely resembles a hovering hummingbird, both in its appearance and its habits. These splendid insects flit from flower to flower on whirring wings, sipping the nectar, just like their avian counterparts. It is not quite as large as a real hummingbird, but nevertheless it is noticeable enough to confuse observers into thinking that they are watching a bird instead of an insect.

Like red admirals and painted ladies, hummingbird hawkmoths originate in Spain and North Africa and head northwards from May onwards, when they are often seen feeding on exotic flowers (including buddleia) in our gardens, especially in the southwest of Britain. Once quite rare here, sightings of hummingbird hawkmoths have increased dramatically in recent years, and the species is now a regular sight from late spring to the end of summer.

PREVIOUS PAGES: The marbled white butterfly is well camouflaged amongst the seedheads of grasses in meadows; often they are only noticed by passersby as they fly up from their roosting points as the grasses are disturbed.

OPPOSITE: The hummingbird hawkmoth is one of the most bizarre and surprising British insects, hovering over flowers like its exotic namesake to suck their nectar.

The hummingbird hawkmoth is noticeable enough to confuse observers into thinking they are watching a bird instead of an insect.

Hedgerows through the seasons

Our hedgerows are home to a huge array of wildlife throughout the year. Hedges often act as useful divisions between areas of farmland but they also provide a safe corridor through which numerous birds, small mammals and invertebrates can travel. A healthy flowering hedge will provide nectar for insects in spring and juicy berries in autumn, and its mass of branches offer shelter through the seasons, particularly in the crucial months of hibernation and breeding.

Mild, fine evenings
from mid-to-late April
onwards usually see the
first bats emerging from
their winter dens.

Fly by night

Britain may have fewer than 60 different kinds of butterfly (a poor showing compared with the hundreds of species found in continental Europe) but we can boast more than 2,400 different kinds of moth. And although a few of these are on the wing during the winter months, the main emergence of moths occurs from April and May onwards.

The vast majority of moths are nocturnal, so we usually spot them either when driving home at night, illuminated in the car headlights; or if we leave a light on and a window open at home, and find moths that have ventured indoors.

Moths, like butterflies, have a fascinating lifecycle which involves four distinct stages: egg, caterpillar, pupa and adult. As with butterflies, the caterpillars of various moth species depend on different food plants, which in turn dictates when the adults are on the wing. Common spring species include the brindled beauty, with its subtle brown and grey markings and triangular shape; Hebrew character, with a distinctive mark on its upperwing that looks like a letter of the Hebrew alphabet; and brimstone moth which, with its yellow colouration, resembles a smaller version of its butterfly namesake.

As the season goes on, many other species begin to emerge, including the various yellow underwings: larger moths which appear brown when their wings are closed, but as their name suggests reveal bright yellow on their hindwings when in flight. These species – especially the common large yellow underwing – provide much of the diet of another suite of nocturnal creatures: bats.

Britain has fewer than 20 species of bat, which is a very small number compared with about 50 species in Europe and more than 1,200 in the world. Some, such as Bechstein's, Leisler's and Natterer's bats, and the two species of horseshoe bat (greater and lesser), have a very localised range; while others, including common and soprano pipistrelles, and the noctule (Britain's largest bat) are common and widespread.

Mild, fine evenings from mid-to-late April onwards usually see the first bats emerging from their winter dens, where they have hibernated for up to six months. They usually come out at dusk, flitting through the chill air in search of flying insects, including moths. Bats use echolocation – a kind of natural sonar – to avoid bumping into objects such as walls and trees and to hunt their prey. Using a series of clicks, they 'bounce' the sound off objects to work out both the nature and size of the object and where it is, even when it is moving!

Once a bat has sensed a yellow underwing moth as it flutters through the night air, it heads for its victim, grabbing it with its claws and transferring it with a single, practised movement into its jaws. The moth never knows what hit it!

The brown long-eared bat uses its extraordinary ears as a tool to hunt its prey, in a technique known as echolocation.

Damsels and dragons

Two closely related groups of insects – dragonflies and damselflies, collectively known by the scientific name *Odonata* – are classic spring and summer creatures. They first appear on warm, sunny days from early April onwards, are at their peak in late spring and summer (from June through to August), and then stay with us until the last rays of sunshine of an Indian summer are over.

The first to appear are usually species from the smaller group, known as damselflies. These are generally about 3–4 centimetres long, with a thin body (the abdomen), a slightly thicker thorax, and a head with extremely large, complex eyes. Damselflies perch with their wings held along their body, which is an easy way (along with their generally far smaller size) to tell them apart from similar-looking dragonflies, which perch with their wings held out at right angles to their body.

The earliest species of damselfly to appear is usually the large red: which may venture out as early as April, though most appear in May. As its name suggests, the large red is a deep crimson colour, with variable amounts of black on the final segments of the abdomen. It can be found throughout Britain on ponds, ditches, canals and bogs, as far north as the Orkney Islands.

By May many of the other common damselflies are beginning to emerge too: the azure, common blue, blue-tailed and the red-eyed (whose eyes really do look like tiny cherry tomatoes stuck to the sides of its head!).

Later, in June, the rest of Britain's twenty or so kinds of damselfly appear. These include several species, such as the willow emerald and dainty damselfly, which have only recently colonised (or in some cases recolonised) Britain, probably as a result of global warming which has enabled them to extend their ranges north and west from continental Europe.

Amongst the damselflies are two species, the banded and beautiful demoiselles, which are often mistaken for dragonflies (or even butterflies) because of their much larger size and more striking appearance than the other damsels. Both species are found on rivers and streams – the aptly-named beautiful demoiselle prefers acid waters and so it is found more frequently in the west

OPPOSITE: The hairy dragonfly is so-called because of its distinctive hairy thorax. Once uncommon, their numbers are increasing throughout England, Ireland and Wales.

BELOW: The azure damselfly is one of the commonest and most widespread of all our springtime insects.

of Britain – where they perform their astonishing fluttering flights on warm sunny days.

Both species have bright metallic green bodies (which appears as a bluer shade in the male), but they can be easily told apart by their wing patterns: the banded has contrasting clear and dark bands, while the beautiful demoiselle's wings are all dark in the male and uniformly pale in the female.

Dragonflies tend to appear later in the year than damselflies, being more associated with the high-summer months of July and August, but there is one notable exception. The hairy dragonfly – so-called because of the fine downy hairs on its thorax – is usually seen from early May, but it will also emerge on fine days in mid-April.

> Mayflies' predators include fish such as pike and trout, and waterbirds such as grey wagtails, which flutter over the surface of the water to grab this free meal.

Mayflies appear, as their name suggests, in the month of May – often emerging en masse to provide a welcome burst of easily available food for a wide range of water creatures. Their predators include fish such as pike and trout, and waterbirds such as grey wagtails, which flutter over the surface of the water to grab this free meal as the adult mayflies emerge. Mayflies proverbially only live for a day, and appropriately they belong to a group of insects known as *ephemeroptera,* from two Greek words meaning 'short-lived' and 'wing'.

All these flying insects provide a useful source of food for one of our most spectacular summer migrants: the hobby. This streamlined falcon, with gunmetal-grey upperparts, creamy underparts streaked with black, and a characteristic orange patch beneath its tail, winters in Africa and arrives back in southern Britain in late April and early May.

The hobby was once a very rare breeding bird in Britain, with fewer than 100 pairs recorded, which were mainly confined to the New Forest and Salisbury Plain. But in recent years its numbers have increased dramatically, and on fine spring days 50 or more birds may gather at wetlands in southern England, where they hunt acrobatically for damselflies and other insects, catching them in mid-air.

A brown trout leaps from the surface of a pond to seize an unwary mayfly.

WHALES & DOLPHINS

It might come as a surprise to learn that many whales, dolphins and porpoises are just as at home in British waters as they are in more exotic Atlantic locations. Around our 9,040 miles of coastline there are over 25 species of these mammals (collectively known as cetaceans) with many more occasional, seasonal visitors too.

Most are commonly found in deep water, only occasionally venturing into shallower waters, but some will swim closer to the shore. Minke whales, porpoises and bottlenose dolphins are all easily viewed from land while others, such as the pilot whale, white-beaked dolphin and the killer whale require a boat trip for a sighting.

Five species of true dolphin live here: the bottle-nosed, common, striped, Atlantic white-sided and white-beaked. We also play host to several species of baleen whales (so-called because instead of teeth their mouths have baleen plates which sift out tiny creatures), including the huge fin whale and its smaller relative, the minke. Our resident toothed whales include the solitary sperm whale, as well as the more sociable pilot and the orca, or killer whale.

The best locations for cetacean spotting are off the Scottish and Welsh/Northern Irish coastline, but dolphins have also been sighted further south in the seas around Dorset and Cornwall.

Nest invaders

Of all our regularly occurring birds of prey, surely the oddest must be the honey buzzard. Unlike the other species of buzzards, hawks and eagles, which mainly feed on mammals and birds, the honey buzzard prefers to dine on wasp larvae, which it obtains by the rather risky procedure of raiding the wasps' nests.

Although very similar at first sight to the common buzzard, the honey buzzard has a smaller head (often described as 'pigeon-like'), and in flight it has a longer tail and holds its wings straight out from its body rather than tilted upwards like the buzzard. Close up, the smaller, greyer head and delicate bill are distinctive.

Despite its name, and superficial resemblance, the honey buzzard is not closely related to the true buzzards, but is in a genus of its own. It is also, like the osprey, hobby and Montagu's harrier, a summer visitor to Britain and Europe, arriving in mid-May and heading back to its winter quarters in equatorial Africa in August or September.

Even when it is here, the honey buzzard is a remarkably difficult bird to see. It has a mainly southerly and westerly distribution, with breeding strongholds in the New Forest, Forest of Dean and Welsh woodlands, although a few pairs do breed as far north in Britain as the Lake District and the Scottish Highlands.

Soon after arriving in May, pairs engage in an aerial display over the forest canopy; but once they have cemented their bond they then retreat into the woods. Here they spend the rest of the spring and summer raising a brood of two chicks, which they feed on the larvae of wasps and bees. Honey buzzards are specially adapted to this dangerous task, with toughened feathers around their bill, which the wasps' stings cannot penetrate, and strong claws enabling them to dig out the nest to reach the larvae in the first place.

There may be fewer than 100 pairs of honey buzzards breeding in Britain, as we are on the very edge of their range; but across the rest of Europe and western Asia this is a very numerous bird indeed.

Like other migrant raptors, honey buzzards struggle to cross large, open areas of water such as the Mediterranean and Red Seas, so they gather in vast flocks above crossing points: the Straits of Gibraltar in the west, and Eilat (in southern Israel) and the Bosphorus (by Istanbul in Turkey) in the east. There it is not unusual for tens of thousands – occasionally more than 100,000 – honey buzzards to pass overhead in a single day.

We cannot yet boast anything like such numbers in the UK, but if global climate change does, as some have predicted, bring warmer summers, this species may become a more frequent sight over our woodlands.

If global climate change does bring warmer summers, the honey buzzard may become a more frequent sight over our woodlands.

The honey buzzard is a summer visitor to our shores, coming from Africa. It feeds itself and its young not on honey, but on the tasty and nutritious grubs of bees and wasps.

Back from the brink

The sight of an otter as it swims rapidly along a river, scurries along the bank, or floats amongst the seaweed offshore, is always a privilege. Few other mammals are so well adapted to a life spent both on water and on land as the otter. Its shapely body covered with dense fur enables it to swim at great speed, and dive beneath the surface of the water in pursuit of fish, while also enabling it to live part of its life on land.

Otters generally mate in early spring: the male or 'dog' otter pursues the female until she finally gives in to his demands. However, she is not entirely submissive – like boxing hares, by testing his stamina she is also ensuring that he is a suitable mate and is carrying the best genetic material she could hope for for her offspring.

Although otters can give birth at any time of year, coastal residents usually do so from May to August, as this coincides with the highest availability of food. Females produce a litter of two or three cubs from May onwards, in a den by a riverbank known as a 'holt'. Like the offspring of many mammals, the cubs are born blind and helpless, and only about 10–12 centimetres long; but thanks to their mother's rich and fatty milk they grow very rapidly, and usually begin to swim by the age of three months or so.

After decades of decline and persecution, otters are now an increasingly familiar sight as this charismatic aquatic mammal returns to much of its former range.

During this period they stay close to their mother, learning to hunt for a range of prey including fish (especially eels), waterbirds such as ducklings and moorhen chicks, and amphibians such as frogs and toads. They have few natural enemies (apart from human beings), but nevertheless they suffer high mortality, especially once they leave the safety of their mother's care the following spring. Many are run over by road vehicles, while others may drown if they are caught in cast-off netting or fishing line.

Otters have undergone an extraordinary fall and rise in their fortunes over the past few years. Because they primarily hunt and feed on fish, they have never been popular with anglers and commercial fishing interests. This is not only so on rivers but also along the coast, where many otters make their home. These coastal otters tend to be less nocturnal than their river-based cousins, as the availability of prey is more closely linked with tides than with diurnal rhythms.

During the period following the Second World War otters were ruthlessly persecuted, both by trapping and shooting, and through hunting, using packs of otterhounds to pursue the animal and kill it. This era also saw major changes to our river systems: pollution from heavy industry, agricultural chemicals and sewage turned some British rivers into death-traps for many aquatic creatures; but being at the top of the food chain, otters suffered more than most.

Gradually these animals began to disappear from major river systems, and although they did hang on around rocky coasts, where there was less pollution and persecution, the population plummeted. In England, the otter virtually disappeared; and even where the creature still hung on, it was almost impossible to see – only the evidence of its droppings (known as 'spraints') gave any indication that it survived at all.

Unlike many iconic British creatures, however, the otter managed to bounce back. In the past few decades numbers have increased to an overall population of more than 10,000 animals; and although Scotland's rivers and coasts remain its stronghold, otters can now be found in every English county. Otters have also taken advantage of the cleanliness of urban rivers such as the Tyne, Tees and Thames and the availability of food there, so that they can now be found in many major cities.

Fantastic Mr Fox?

Another now-familiar sight in the cities is the fox. During the spring months, fox populations multiply in town and country, emerging along with other baby mammals that leave the safety of their den for the wider world at the same time.

The undeniably cute fox cubs are born in litters of four or five during March, April and May. Blind and helpless at first, they are fed with their mother's milk and grow rapidly, being weaned after about four weeks. At this stage in their lives they are easy to see, especially because, like all baby animals, these cubs are keen to explore their exciting new environment and also indulge in play.

Play-fights between siblings are an important way for cubs to learn vital techniques that they will later use to hunt prey and to deal with rivals. They also give us the ideal opportunity to watch fascinating (and very endearing) behaviour, often at close quarters. At this stage the cubs have not learned to fear human beings, so they may be very approachable.

Of course, not everyone likes foxes. Indeed, with the possible exception of the badger, the fox is our most controversial mammal. Few other wild animals polarise opinion as much as the fox: and the division of views is also often a reflection of the division between town and country. On the one hand, many farmers, gamekeepers and other country-dwellers loathe foxes with a determined intensity for their ability to break into chicken coops and wreak havoc on the unfortunate occupants. On the other hand, city-dwellers often regard the fox with a degree of affection; perhaps recognising it as a kindred spirit, which like them has adapted its behaviour to living in the urban jungle. Indeed, for many urban Britons the fox is – with the exception of the non-native grey squirrel – the only wild mammal they ever normally see.

Town and country foxes behave differently, too. No doubt the shyness of rural foxes is a learned behaviour, following centuries of persecution, which they need to maintain if they are to survive. Foxhunting may now be illegal, but shooting foxes is not; and if a country fox strays within range of a shotgun usually it will not survive for very long. In contrast, urban foxes seem to have no fear; in most British cities you may encounter a fox at any time of day or night, often strolling unfazed along a busy street. While some people fear the presence of this clearly predatory mammal, others enjoy this reminder of the countryside in the town.

However urban foxes are not popular with everyone: well-publicised stories about alleged attacks on children and dogs (which may happen, but are extremely rare) have led to calls for fox culls in cities. Foxes are also

Foxes often fight over territorial boundaries and food, especially in our towns and cities where their territories are more closely packed than in the countryside. The fox on the left is adopting a submissive pose.

blamed for making a mess while raiding dustbins for food, and for keeping people awake with their blood-curdling mating calls during December and February.

Once she has mated, the female fox (vixen) seeks out a safe place to make her den, known as an earth. In the countryside foxes often use old badger setts or simply dig a hole into an earth bank in a wood. Towns and cities offer a wider range of potential locations for dens, including churchyards and cemeteries (often fairly undisturbed and with plenty of nooks and crannies where they can hide away); cuttings on active and disused railway lines, which also act as useful corridors for the foxes to move through their hunting territory; and of course domestic gardens.

Foxes often make their earth beneath a garden shed or other outbuilding, which offers the ideal combination of a ready-made hiding place and also plenty of food – both of the wild variety and that provided accidentally or deliberately by us. As the spring and summer progresses, fox cubs become more wary, and also begin to wander farther afield. The males are usually first to leave the safety of their mother's care, and as a result suffer a very high mortality rate. Female cubs tend to hang around the earth longer, but both males and females have usually left by the autumn, as by then they are almost fully-grown and have become potential rivals to their parents. And so the cycle continues...

As spring and summer
progresses, fox cubs
become more wary, and
also begin to wander
further afield.

Life below ground

Alongside the fox sits another mammal that is much-loved in children's literature, and which has also become a controversial creature in modern times.

The recent debate over the role of badgers in spreading bovine tuberculosis amongst cattle has obscured, and in many ways tainted, our understanding of Britain's largest terrestrial mammalian predator.

Badgers have had a long and complex relationship with humans. Like so many predators, they were ruthlessly persecuted during the nineteenth century because they ate the eggs and chicks of ground-nesting gamebirds, and also competed with foxes for earths, which made them unpopular with foxhunters. Also around this time the newly invented shotgun enabled farmers and gamekeepers to shoot them far more easily than before. Badger-baiting – the digging out of a badger from a sett using spades and specially trained dogs – was also rife, and still occurs in some parts of the country despite the fact that it has been illegal since Victorian times.

But their popularity was undoubtedly given a boost – along with that of the mole and water vole – by the publication in 1908 of Kenneth Grahame's celebrated and much-loved children's book *The Wind in the Willows*. Grahame's portrayal of the badger as a stern but kindly old gentleman, living peacefully in the middle of the Wild Wood and enjoying an adventure with his friends Ratty and Mole, helped to create a positive and endearing image of the badger, which despite the recent controversy over bovine TB, continues to this day.

So if we can set aside our prejudices for or against the badger, there can be no argument that this is one of our most fascinating wild animals.

Although it does not resemble them in appearance, the badger is one of the mustelids, which means it is related to the otter, stoat, weasel, pine marten and polecat, and also to the introduced and non-native mink. Yet this creature has taken a very different evolutionary route from these slender, streamlined animals: both in shape and their feeding habits, badgers are more like armadillos or anteaters than otters or weasels – being mainly foragers rather than predators.

In terms of their prey and diet badgers are generalists rather than specialists, feeding on a wide range of animal and plant material, including beetles, fruit, rodents, hedgehogs and small birds (and their eggs). However, their preferred food is earthworms, which they dig out of the ground using their sharp, powerful claws.

Unlike most carnivores, badgers are social animals, living together in communities of two dozen or so adults in large, underground networks of

Badgers are largely nocturnal mammals so they are rarely seen, though in some areas they now regularly appear in gardens in search of food.

tunnels and 'rooms' known as setts. Some badger setts are incredibly old, going back hundreds of years, while others may be much more recent in origin. In many cases the same dynasty of badgers has inhabited a sett for many generations, though new animals do arrive and established ones depart from time to time.

Whereas foxes have moved relatively recently into our towns and cities in search of food and a new place to raise a family, urban badgers will have been in their current location long before the city grew up around them. Leafy cities with plenty of green corridors, such as London, Bristol and Brighton, are especially good for badgers because they offer plenty of opportunities for feeding in parks and gardens, though increased disturbance from human beings, or development for housing, roads or industry, has led some urban setts to fall into decline.

> Kenneth Grahame's portrayal of the badger as a stern but kindly old gentleman, living peacefully in the middle of the Wild Wood and enjoying an adventure with his friends Ratty and Mole, helped to create a positive and endearing image of the badger.

Badgers breed using a technique known as 'delayed implantation'. This means that after mating the fertilised egg is not implanted into the female badger's womb until much later in the year – usually in December. After a pregnancy lasting six or seven weeks, she gives birth in February, to a litter of between one and three (occasionally as many as five) cubs. The young remain in the safety of the sett for another eight weeks or so, finally emerging above ground some time in April. The female may then mate again immediately, or wait until the autumn to do so.

At this time of year, having raised a family of cubs, badgers often 'spring-clean' their setts, and piles of grass and other plant foliage can sometimes be seen by the entrance holes, this used bedding discarded in favour of fresh new material.

Badgers are long-lived creatures, surviving on average about eight years, though some may live twice as long as that. However, most badgers you will find at a particular sett are likely to be youngsters, as badgers suffer a very heavy mortality rate from road traffic, with as many as 50,000 being killed each year out of a total UK population of about 300,000 animals. Despite this, badgers are on now on the increase: their numbers having almost doubled from the mid-1980s to the 1990s.

OPPOSITE: The mole is one of our commonest mammals, yet because of its subterranean habits it is hardly ever seen above ground.

FOLLOWING PAGES: In 1988 DEFRA revealed that after an absence of hundreds of years, the wild boar was back and roaming the wilds of Britain.

Grappling giants

Britain's largest beetle, reaching a length of up to 9 centimetres, the stag beetle is also one of the most fearsome-looking British insects. The name comes, of course, from the huge claws, resembling deer antlers, which the beetle uses – just like deer stags – to fight rival males over the chance to mate with the females. Two male stag beetles locking their claws together, each trying to overturn their opponent in the insect equivalent of all-in wrestling, is a truly extraordinary sight, though one that is witnessed less often nowadays as this species declines here.

Stag beetles also have an extraordinary lifecycle. Having mated, the female seeks out a dead tree trunk or branch where she will lay her eggs and then die. Soon afterwards, the cream-coloured grubs hatch out, then live and feed inside the rotting wood for up to six years. Once fully grown, the grub then heads downwards into the soil beneath, where it turns into a pupa, in which state it remains during the winter and spring. The following summer the adult beetle finally emerges for its brief few weeks of glory.

Stag beetles are one of our largest and most impressive insects. They get their name from the huge, antler-like horns on the male's head which they use in combat to win a watching female – just like their much larger namesake, the deer stag.

With such a complex lifecycle, it is hardly surprising that numbers of stag beetles have declined in recent years, as much dead and dying wood is removed in the process of 'tidying up' parks and gardens, or on health and safety grounds. Fortunately, the importance of dead wood to stag beetles has now been recognised, and conservationists are doing their best to encourage people to retain or recreate the ideal habitats for these creatures. Gardens are especially important, as more than half of all sightings of this giant insect occur there.

Stag beetles are only on the wing for a few weeks, usually from the very end of May or early June into July or August, but nevertheless their large size and habit of flying around on warm summer evenings in urban and suburban areas means that people often notice them.

London is their main UK stronghold, as its south-easterly geographical position and the 'urban heat-island' effect means that average spring and summer temperatures there are noticeably warmer than elsewhere in the country. However, the city streets are also a dangerous place for this big beetle, as they often bask on warm pavements to heat up their bodies, and get accidentally – or sometimes deliberately – crushed by pedestrians.

Weather words

'Oak before ash, we're in for a splash;
ash before oak, we're in for a soak.'

This ancient rhyme was coined by our distant ancestors who did not have the benefit of satellites, supercomputers and other high-tech forecasting aids to help them predict the weather. Instead, they looked around them and observed the seasonal changes in nature to determine a long-term weather forecast.

The rhyme suggests that when oak buds come into leaf before those of the ash – which usually happens during a fine, settled spring – the rainfall over the rest of the season will be fairly minimal: just a 'splash'. But if the black, sticky buds of the ash burst into leaf before those of the oak, we should expect heavy downpours and prolonged spells of unsettled, rainy weather.

In the past, oak leaves appeared, on average, four or five days before those of the ash, in keeping with the pattern of generally dry weather during May and June. But in recent years a shift in spring climate patterns has led to the oak coming into leaf far earlier: on average a full two weeks earlier, usually by mid-April. The ash has also shifted earlier, but only by about nine days.

If the proverb is correct, this should mean that we are in for a long run of dry, settled springs. On the other hand, we might take this with a pinch of salt!

Another famous weather proverb refers to the arrival of spring blossom:

'Ne'er cast a clout till may is out.'

Many people mistakenly assume that this means, 'Don't leave your coat at home until the month of May is over'. In fact 'may' here is the common name of one of our hedgerow plants, the hawthorn, and this proverb refers to its fluffy white blossom, warning us not to take off our winter clothes until it has appeared.

Once again, this date is shifting earlier and earlier in the calendar: as its folk-name suggests, hawthorn used to come into flower in the month of May; nowadays, especially in southern Britain, it usually appears by the middle of April. Another well-known hedgerow plant flowers later than both hawthorn and blackthorn. The characteristic creamy, flat blossoms of the elder usually appear in late May or June, towards the end of spring. By June, most of the plants in a typical hedgerow are in full leaf and flower.

Scientists have discovered that if you count the number of different kinds of woody plant along a 27-metre stretch of hedgerow, you can work out the approximate date of that hedge in centuries. So, five or six different species means the hedge was planted five or six centuries ago.

A tree sparrow perches amongst a flurry of white hawthorn blossom, a classic sign of spring.

Weathering a change

The contrasting fortunes of two of our woodland breeding species are helping to reveal the effects of global climate change on Britain's wildlife.

The great tit and pied flycatcher are small-to-medium-sized songbirds, and both nest in holes in trees in our ancient woodlands, with the great tit having also moved into gardens. The two species readily take to artificial nestboxes as convenient substitutes for natural holes, which may be hard to find.

The great tit, like the other members of its family, is a resident species, found here all the year round, but the pied flycatcher, like its cousin the spotted flycatcher and a range of other insect-eating birds, such as warblers and chats, is a migrant, wintering mainly in West Africa. Sometime in early spring, pied flycatchers begin the long journey back north, arriving on their breeding grounds – mainly in the western oakwoods of England, Wales and Scotland – from mid-April until early May.

As with many long-distance migrant birds, male pied flycatchers arrive back a few days earlier than females. This enables them to grab the best territories so that when the females do return they can choose their mates and get down to breeding.

But during the past three decades or so, the timing of spring in Britain has advanced, on average, by between one and three weeks. Different species have responded to this change in very different ways; and the moth caterpillars on which both great tits and pied flycatchers feed their young are now emerging several weeks earlier than they used to. Once they have appeared, they are also taking advantage of the more benevolent conditions to grow more quickly, which in turn leads them to pupate more rapidly.

All this means that the birds that depend on them – including the great tit and pied flycatcher – have also had to change their habits. They must start nesting and laying their eggs earlier than before, so that when the chicks hatch there are plenty of caterpillars available. And they need a lot of them: the average pair of great tits will bring back up to 1,000 caterpillars every single day!

Being resident birds, great tits have managed to adapt their breeding behaviour to start the cycle earlier – by as much as two weeks in some populations – so that they are still in synchronisation with the main emergence of the caterpillars.

But because pied flycatchers are migrants, whose arrival is generally triggered by the changes in day length in Africa (which happens at the same time every year), they have struggled to adapt. Although some European populations (especially those in the far north such as Finland and Sweden) have begun to migrate and breed earlier, the British ones have not; which has led to a sharp decline in their breeding success.

Having increased in numbers in the two decades between the first and second BTO Atlas surveys (from 1968–72 to 1988–91), largely due to the provision of artificial nestboxes, the pied flycatcher population has dropped sharply since the mid-1990s. Today, the species is on the Amber List of threatened birds, having declined by between 25 per cent and 50 per cent since then.

If climate change continues to accelerate, as has been predicted, the combination of even earlier springs and the increase in extreme weather events (such as storms and floods) could drive the numbers of the pied flycatcher population even lower.

OPPOSITE: The pied flycatcher is a spring visitor to our shores, arriving here early in the season. The male (right) will arrive slightly earlier than the female (left) to pick the best territories in their breeding ground.

BELOW: Great tits are highly adaptable birds, taking readily to nesting in artificial boxes when holes in trees are in short supply.

Seasonal seabirds

Britain is justly famous for its teeming seabird colonies which line rocky cliffs, headlands and offshore islands around much of our coastline, especially in the north and west. These vast gatherings of birds, full of activity, sounds and smells, have b een described as 'Britain's Serengeti', a natural spectacle to rival any in the world.

Yet for more than half the year, from August through to March, the cliff ledges and tops are devoid of life. The birds that breed there vanish, in many cases travelling hundreds or even thousands of miles from our shores. Until very recently the exact whereabouts of many of our seabirds – even familiar species such as the puffin – remained a mystery when they weren't in Britain.

But thanks to satellite technology, which allows scientists to place an unobtrusive tracking device onto the birds and follow their global journeys, we now have a more specific idea of where they spend the autumn and winter months. Puffins, for example, head out into a desolate and featureless stretch of the North Atlantic and live at sea for months on end.

So why do they come here at all? The obvious answer is that although they depend on the sea for much of the year, they obviously cannot lay their eggs and raise their young there! They choose Britain partly because we are surrounded by very fertile and productive seas where they can find food for themselves and their chicks; but also because our coastline provides the ideal habitat.

Nesting in such high densities makes these colonies of seabirds vulnerable to terrestrial predators such as foxes, rats and domestic cats; so they usually choose to nest on remote cliff faces, often on offshore islands where there are no land-based predators. Britain has a wealth of such island groups, including Shetland, Orkney and the Western Isles in Scotland, along with smaller ones such as the Farne Islands off Northumberland, and the Pembrokeshire islands of Skomer, Skokholm and Grassholm.

Seabirds mostly return to their British breeding grounds from March onwards, and immediately they begin to establish a territory, jostling for the best position with their fellow birds. Unlike birds of prey, whose territory may range over several hundred square miles, those of cliff-nesting auks such as the guillemot and razorbill are the smallest in the bird world – covering just a few square feet.

This means that they are living cheek by jowl with their neighbours, which can lead to plenty of squabbling. To avoid the skirmishes escalating into full-blown conflict, many seabirds have evolved special displays of controlled aggression, such as lifting their heads up and calling loudly, which enable them to keep to their places with honour satisfied on both sides, and waste less energy in fights.

Puffins may look comical in flight or on the ground, but they are masters of hunting underwater for their favourite food, sand eels.

Seabirds mostly return to their British breeding grounds from March onwards, and immediately they begin to establish a territory.

For the first few weeks after their territory is established, the birds fly offshore to find food. The fact that they are unable to defend this unpredictable and peripatetic food supply – unlike most other land-nesting birds – is another reason why they are able to nest in such close contact with each other.

Different species of seabird choose different places to breed. The cliff ledges are the preserve of guillemots and razorbills, together with the kittiwake, an ocean-going gull. Kittiwakes can be identified by their grey and white plumage, yellow-green bill, black legs, and in flight by their black wingtips, which look as if they have been dipped in ink.

Guillemots and razorbills are superficially similar in appearance – both chunky little birds, dark above and white below, with short, stubby wings and a characteristic upright stance rather like a miniature penguin. A closer look reveals that the razorbill is much darker than its cousin – almost black – and has a thick bill with a straight edge and curved end, shaped rather like an old-fashioned razor, while the guillemot's bill is slender and pointed.

The grassy areas at the tops of the cliffs are home to the fulmar – a bird that superficially resembles a gull but, unlike gulls, which rarely venture far out to sea, has the tube-nosed bill of a true seabird, a device that enables it to expel salt from seawater. On some islands these areas also support puffins – whose brightly coloured bill and comical appearance makes it the nation's favourite seabird – which make their nests in old rabbit burrows.

Our largest seabird, the gannet, breeds in vast and noisy colonies such as Bass Rock in the Firth of Forth off Edinburgh, the Welsh island of Grassholm, and St Kilda off northwest Scotland. From their rocky nest-sites these huge white birds head out to sea to find shoals of fish, then plunge down into the water at speeds of up to 100 kph (more than 60 mph) to seize their unsuspecting prey.

Two groups of seabirds related to one another – gulls and terns – tend to live along the coast rather than out at sea compared with other, more marine species, but will often nest alongside them. In the gulls' case this enables them to predate on smaller birds, taking eggs, chicks and even, on occasion, full-grown adults.

Their close relatives, great and Arctic skuas, have taken this to new lengths: as well as killing their neighbours they also harry them in the air to make them regurgitate and drop their food, a habit known as kleptoparasitism (see page 178).

If the smaller seabirds do manage to raise their chick (usually one, though sometimes more) to the point where it can leave the nest, this is where the danger really begins. Guillemot parents must persuade – or in many cases force – their reluctant chicks to jump off the cliff ledge into the sea below, a drop of some distance. At this stage the young guillemot has not even fledged, and cannot yet fly; but it is still safer on the water with its parents than on the ledge, where a passing gull or skua may grab it.

OPPOSITE: Gannets are well known for their faithfulness to their mate. Every year they renew their bond by facing each other and pointing their heads up to the sky together in an elegant display of love and loyalty.

FOLLOWING PAGES: Basking sharks are the second largest fish in the world, yet are entirely harmless, feeding on plankton in our fertile offshore waters during the summer months.

Commotion in the ocean

As the temperatures on land begin to warm up, in the weeks following the spring equinox, so this process is mirrored in the seas and oceans surrounding the British Isles. However, because the sea acts like a kind of giant storage heater, being warmer than the land in winter and cooler in summer, the timing of events is not quite the same for our marine wildlife as for terrestrial creatures.

The waters around the UK are mainly shallow, rarely reaching depths of more than 100 metres, and much shallower close to the coastline. This allows plenty of sunlight to permeate the water, which in turn means that our seas are amongst the richest in terms of marine life of any in the world.

Although much of our undersea wildlife is hidden from view, it is no less rich than that on land – indeed, it is arguably even more varied. Rockpools and shorelines support a wealth of fish such as blennies and gobies, which hide in crevices or burrow into the sand to avoid being seen; crustaceans such as shore and edible crabs and shrimps, and molluscs including snails, limpets and barnacles; as well as many varieties of seaweed, which are not actually plants but are multicellular algae.

Further offshore, a wealth of hidden sealife awaits, including all the elements required for a functioning marine ecosystem: tiny plankton, fish and crustaceans

BELOW: Yellow cluster anemones are just one of the many extraordinary sea creatures found under our coastal waters.

OPPOSITE: The tompot blenny is a very inquisitive fish that will make friends with divers it encounters in its home territories around the south and west coasts of Britain.

Seahorses are the only creature on Earth in which the male experiences a true pregnancy.

of all shapes and sizes, and seabirds. At the top of the food chain, there are the big predators: seals, sharks and cetaceans (whales, dolphins and porpoises).

From April onwards, the marine ecosystem bursts into life, as the higher temperatures mean that millions of birds and marine mammals that have wintered far away from our shores return to feed and breed. And amongst them is one tiny creature you might not expect to find off our coasts: the seahorse.

Seahorses are truly amazing creatures. As their name suggests, they resemble tiny horses, though they are actually fish. They swim in a vertical position, using their long, prehensile tail rather like a miniature monkey would, to anchor themselves to underwater foliage and prevent themselves being swept out to sea by tides and strong currents.

Their other claim to fame is that seahorses are the only creature on Earth in which the male experiences a true pregnancy, keeping hundreds of eggs in his pouch until they hatch out into tiny young during the spring.

Two species of seahorse – spiny and short-snouted – can be found in British waters, mainly off our southern coasts. The major stronghold is in Dorset's Studland Bay, whose calm, warm waters are ideal for the growth of seagrass, the habitat these tiny fish need in order to breed.

Unfortunately, being in shallow waters just offshore from a major tourist hotspot, this is also one of the most disturbed marine habitats in Britain. Conservationists are now working closely with the tourism, fishing and boating industries to ensure that the seahorses' precious habitat remains safe and undamaged, and that these extraordinary and unique creatures survive.

OPPOSITE: Seahorses may look tropical, but they live in the cold waters off our shores, with their main stronghold off the south coast of England.

ABOVE: Like its relatives, the velvet swimming crab protects itself using its hard shell and fearsome claws.

SUMMER
INTO
AUTUMN

The lazy, hazy days of high summer sometimes feel as if they will never end. The low hum of insects, the scent of wild flowers and the shimmering heat haze bely the stark truth: that autumn will soon be here, a season which brings with it huge challenges for our wildlife. Until that time, millions of young birds and mammals enjoy the warmer months as they leave the safety of their nests and dens and explore the big wide world. Our woods, fields and meadows are awash with colour as trees, shrubs and flowers reach their glorious peak, and as summer ends, leaves take on rich autumnal shades while plants fruit or set seed for the next stage in their cycle and to feed hungry animals in the season to come.

AT THE MONUMENT of Stonehenge, on the edge of one of southern England's last great wildernesses, Salisbury Plain, a motley group of people assemble around the ancient stones to wait for sunrise.

They have come, as they and their ancestors have done for centuries, to mark the high point of the solar calendar: the Summer Solstice. This is the Longest Day, when the Northern Hemisphere experiences more hours of daylight than at any other time of year. Varying between 20 and 22 June from year to year, this also marks 'Midsummer's Day': not, as is often assumed, the 'middle of summer', but from the Germanic 'mid', meaning 'with' – i.e. the day when summer finally arrives.

Although this is the moment when the days begin to shorten as we approach autumn, the temperatures continue to rise for some time yet, usually peaking towards the end of July or the beginning of August, and reaching the mid- or, on rare occasions, the high thirty degrees Celsius.

For most of Britain's wildlife, this is a time both of plenty and of leisure. Birds have mostly fledged their chicks, mammals have raised their kits, cubs and pups, and insects are on the wing. Nature is in full flow, with vegetation – trees, bushes and wild flowers – at its fullest, as every hedgerow, field and verge is awash with green, dotted with splashes of colour.

Because most birds and mammals have by now raised a family, the total number of individual creatures is at its peak. Chicks may have left the safety of their nests, but they still need their parents, and they cheep frantically

as they beg for morsels of food. Fox cubs frolic in city gardens and country churchyards; baby rabbits chase around their warrens; and badgers emerge from their setts at dusk to forage for worms. On the high tops of the Cairngorm plateau, all but a few patches of snow have melted, and the creatures that turned white during the winter – ptarmigan, mountain hare and stoat – are now in their summer garb, which once again allows them to blend into their surroundings.

Marine life reaches its peak at this time of year too: as the waters finally warm up under summer sunshine, whales, dolphins, porpoises and basking sharks are seen off our coasts. And beneath the surface a maelstrom of activity signals the peak in the lifecycles of many smaller sea creatures.

Not every species has finished breeding, though. Around our northern and eastern coasts, common seal pups are born at the height of summer, and are still dependent on their mothers for some time yet; while their larger relatives, grey seals, will not give birth until well into the autumn. Many common birds, such as the blackbird, song thrush and swallow, produce several broods, so even though their first offspring of the year may already be on the wing, the parents are busy incubating another clutch of eggs, or feeding the next hungry brood of young.

One of our best-known pieces of weather folklore, the legend of St Swithun, claims that if it rains or is sunny on 15 July (St Swithun's Day), the same weather will continue for 40 days and 40 nights – more or less up until the August Bank Holiday. In fact our weather is rarely so

consistent, and although we do get summer droughts and floods, a more typical weather pattern follows that famous description of an English summer: two fine days followed by a thunderstorm. In some years, such as the long hot summer of 1976 or the washout of 2012, the prevailing weather can have a considerable effect on wildlife; but usually there is enough food available at this time of year for most creatures to thrive.

By high summer – the holiday season of mid-August, when roads to airports and the seaside grind to a halt – nature begins to quiet. Almost all the birds have stopped singing, and often they appear to have vanished into thin air (in fact they are hiding away to avoid predators as they moult into fresh plumage), while many wild flowers have already bloomed and begun to set seed. The only soundtrack of these lazy days is the low hum of insects; though as populations of bumblebees and butterflies continue to decline, even this is diminishing across much of our countryside.

This may appear to be a time of plenty, but don't be fooled: autumn is just around the corner, and many wild creatures are preparing for a time when finding food will become progressively more difficult. As August gives way to September, we often enjoy a spell of fine, settled weather, a chance for butterflies and dragonflies to stock up on precious energy-giving nectar. Alternatively, in some years the first autumn gales bring summer to an abrupt end, as winds and rain sweep in off the Atlantic.

The drawing in of the nights towards the autumn equinox also triggers a signal in the brains of our migrant birds, impelling them to head south on their epic journeys across the globe. With bird populations swollen by millions of youngsters heading off on their first journey, at this time of year we witness the greatest mass movement of life on Earth.

Nature's vanishing act continues, as the colours of the summer flowers fade and insects disappear, while the trees begin to don their autumnal hues, exchanging various shades of green for more muted yellows, reds and browns. It's not all about disappearance and decline, though: new visitors are just around the corner, as millions of birds arrive from farther north and east for the winter, to take advantage of our milder climate.

But as the revellers gather around Stonehenge to witness the dawn of the summer solstice, all this is still way off in the future. For now, let us embark on the summer season, a time when Nature's bounty is all around us.

The sound of summer

Along with the last tuneful trills from songbirds and the gentle buzz of bumblebees, one of the most characteristic soundtracks of summer is the noise made by millions of crickets and grasshoppers, which echoes along every grassy verge, meadow and hedgerow, especially on fine sunny days.

More often heard than seen, these two closely related groups of insects are easily confused; and indeed they do share many similarities. Both are long-legged insects with incredible leaping abilities; able to escape danger, like Superman, with one enormous bound. Both can be found in a range of habitats, especially in swathes of long, uncut grass, and both share the extraordinary ability to produce a sound so loud it can even, on occasion, keep humans awake.

These sounds are the insect equivalent of birdsong: a key part of their courtship displays, enabling males to attract a mate while at the same time fending off their rivals. But although both grasshoppers and crickets produce sound by the action of rubbing one part of their body against another, they do so in very different ways. Crickets chirp by rubbing their wings together, with the serrated edge of the bottom of one wing passing across the top of the other, like the teeth of a steel comb. The sound produced by this simple action is extraordinary: some crickets can chirp at a volume of between 70 and 100 decibels, equivalent to that of a chainsaw or a pneumatic drill. Grasshoppers employ a different technique, using their hind legs, which they rub against their wings to produce a similar chirping sound. However, because they are mainly diurnal, their sound – though often equal in volume to that of the cricket – is less obvious, as it occurs at a time of day when there are many other natural and manmade sounds competing for our attention.

There are further differences between the two groups. Crickets are generally larger (the great green bush-cricket is one of our longest insects, measuring up to 4.5 centimetres in length, while most grasshoppers are about 1.5 centimetres long) and have longer antennae. Female crickets also have a much longer ovipositor (the tube at the rear of the abdomen through which she lays her eggs).

While grasshoppers have a vegetarian diet, mainly eating grass and other plant material, crickets are not only scavengers but also predators, lying in wait to ambush any passing insect unfortunate enough to cross their path.

Although many crickets are common and widespread, some specialised species are on the edge of their range in Britain, and so are only found in southern counties. One of the rarest is the mole cricket, which like its mammalian namesake lives virtually the whole of its life underground, using its powerful front legs to dig burrows in the soil. In Britain there have only been a handful

PREVIOUS PAGES: The harvest mouse is the only native British mammal that has a prehensive tail which it twists around plant stems to help it climb.

OPPOSITE: The great green bush cricket is one of our longest insects and is a glorious sight when in flight on a summer's day.

of sightings in the past 25 years. It can be identified by its large size (up to 4.5 centimetres long) and brown thorax covered with velvet-like hairs.

Like many other insects, crickets and grasshoppers have a long and complex reproductive cycle which begins in the summer months. Crickets mate towards the end of summer and lay their eggs in the autumn. These then hatch the following spring, in time for the offspring to have the greatest chance of survival. Grasshoppers mate and lay their eggs earlier, at the height of summer. The young of both groups develop by a process of growing and shedding their hard outer shell several times as they do so, until they become fully adult.

Grasshoppers' habit of singing all day has led to a wealth of folktales about them, of which by far the most well-known is Aesop's 'The Ant and the Grasshopper'. In the story, while the ant toils all summer to prepare his winter home and put aside stores of food, the grasshopper wastes the long summer days playing his incessant tune. When the autumn winds begin to blow, and food runs short, the grasshopper realises he has not prepared for the lean times ahead, and begs the ant to give him food and shelter. The ant refuses to help, and the grasshopper starves to death; a salutary tale for any creatures that might be tempted to forget that, even at this time of sunshine and plenty, hard times are just around the corner.

Crickets are predators, lying in wait to ambush any passing insect unfortunate enough to cross their path.

Treasures of the wild

Of all the world's flowers, perhaps the most prized are orchids. They are a diverse groups of plants, with more than 25,000 species found on all continents apart from Antarctica, from the Equator to beyond the Arctic Circle.

Orchid collectors are famously obsessive, and some rare individual specimens can change hands for thousands of dollars. Orchids fascinate both collectors and botanists – and indeed all nature-lovers – because they combine beauty, scarcity and some of the most extraordinary lifecycles of any living thing. They have evolved a wide range of relationships with other organisms: notably by evolving complex floral structures which mimic insects such as bumblebees to fool them into landing on the flower with the intention of mating, thus allowing pollination to take place. A few species have even forsaken the conventional ability of most plants to photosynthesise and instead form a parasitic relationship with fungi, obtaining all their energy by this unusual means.

Although many people think of orchids as being exotic flowers, they can also be found growing wild in Britain: almost 60 species occur here regularly, with some of them relatively common and widespread, especially during their peak flowering period from May through to August.

Orchids prefer unspoilt habitats with relatively poor soils, which includes wildflower meadows, marshland, chalk downland and heathland. These habitats enable the orchids to thrive because they don't have to compete with more vigorously growing grasses. However, many orchid species have declined in numbers in recent years, as more and more of the countryside has disappeared under industrial-scale farmland. In a single season, pesticides and herbicides will kill a colony of orchids that has existed for thousands of years, so these plants are now as likely to form colonies in marginal, forgotten and manmade sites such as former industrial workings and roadside verges as they are in the wider countryside.

Classic midsummer species include common spotted, southern marsh and pyramidal orchids, all of which are fairly widespread in suitable habitats in England and Wales, with the common spotted also found in Scotland. Scarcer, more localised species, such as the early and late spider orchids, man orchid and lizard orchid, have a much more restricted distribution, mainly on the grasslands of southeast England.

Two of our rarest wild flowers are orchids – the lady's slipper, confined to a single, secret site in Yorkshire, which is carefully guarded by conservationists to prevent collectors taking the blooms; and the near-mythical ghost orchid, which has only been recorded once in 25 years, and may now be extinct in Britain.

One of our rarest wild flowers, the lady's slipper orchid, is confined to just one location in Yorkshire, where it grows in secret, protected by conservationists.

Beauty in miniature

High summer sees the emergence of a group of butterflies that may not be as large or as brightly coloured as some of their commoner cousins, but which are nevertheless perfect examples of beauty in miniature. These are the downland butterflies, which appear for a few weeks between June and August on the chalk and limestone grasslands of southern Britain.

These are true specialists, usually laying their eggs on a single kind of plant, on which the caterpillars then feed when they hatch. For this reason these species are very vulnerable to environmental change and many have been in long-term decline since the Second World War, when the process began of converting ancient grasslands into intensive arable farmland.

Since then we have lost more than 90 per cent of this specialised habitat, and that which remains is mostly concentrated in the southern counties of England; from Dorset and Wiltshire in the west, through Hampshire and Surrey, to Kent and Sussex in the east, with some areas also in Devon, Somerset and Gloucestershire.

Chalk downland butterflies come from several different groups, including the skippers, the blues, the fritillaries and the browns. The skippers – such as the dingy, grizzled and silver-spotted – are especially easy to overlook, as they are small and brown and when at rest they hold their wings in a way that resembles several species of day-flying moth.

One of the rarest, the Lulworth skipper, is confined to the short stretch of coast near Lulworth Cove in Dorset, though it is a common and widespread species on the continent. On sunny days in late July and early August the downs above the cove may be thronged with hundreds of thousands of this tiny, olive-coloured insect.

The blues are generally more noticeable, not least because as their name suggests they come in varying shades of blue. The species range from the brightly coloured common blue, through the paler chalkhill blue, to the dazzling Adonis blue, which is one of our most striking summer butterflies. However, the females of several of these species are not blue, but in fact chocolate-brown, while confusingly the males and females of some members of this group, including the exquisite brown Argus and the tiny small blue (our smallest butterfly, with a wingspan of just 18–27 millimetres) are brown or blackish in colour.

The best-known blue is the large blue, which actually became extinct in Britain in 1979. Following its demise, scientists studying large blues in Sweden managed to uncover this butterfly's extraordinary lifecycle. This involves the

The male Adonis blue is one of our most dramatic and beautiful butterflies, outshining its somewhat less dazzling brown-winged female.

caterpillar being 'adopted' by a certain species of red ant, by secreting a sweet, sticky substance that attracts the ants and prompts them to carry the caterpillar down into their nest. Once underground, it feasts on the ant grubs until it finally emerges as an adult the following summer. By this parasitic behaviour, the large blue ensures a safe place in which its offspring can grow, with a guaranteed food supply close at hand.

In order to restore the large blue to our fauna, butterfly conservationists then set about creating the ideal habitat which would meet the needs of each stage of the large blue's lifecycle. This meant providing short-cropped grass to encourage the all-important ants, and wild thyme which would offer up the nectar on which the adults feed. Once these habitats had been established to their satisfaction, conservationists then reintroduced the large blue to these sites in the West Country, where the species is now thriving – although the adults are only on the wing for a brief period of just two or three weeks throughout the months of June and July.

> By its parasitic behaviour, the large blue ensures a safe place in which its offspring can grow, with a guaranteed food supply close at hand.

More widespread chalkland butterflies that you can spot at this time of year include several species of 'brown' butterfly: the black-and-white chequered marbled white, the small heath and the grayling. The latter is a buff-and-brown butterfly which is a master of disguise; it is visible while in flight, but once it rests on the ground and closes its wings to conceal its colourful orange markings it becomes surprisingly hard to see, being perfectly camouflaged against the bare, stony ground. It is often found along grassy paths near coastlines, especially where the soil is sandy and well drained.

Other butterflies often seen on chalk grassland – as well as in many other habitats and even rural gardens – include the exquisite small copper, with its contrasting orange-and-black coloration; and our two most common and widespread butterflies of high summer, the meadow brown, with its dull brown wings and orange markings, and the gatekeeper, also known as the hedge brown, with its bright golden wings.

The marbled white butterfly is a common sight on chalk grasslands in summer. It is easily identified by its dappled brown-and-white coloration.

Pups' progress

For the smaller and (paradoxically, given its name) scarcer of our two native species of seal, summer is the most important time in their lifecycle. This is when common seals give birth to a single pup – the culmination of a complex process that began the previous July, when the male and female mated at sea.

As with several other species of mammal, including the badger, the fertilised egg is not implanted in the mother's womb until three months or so after mating, and only then does the foetus begin to grow. This ensures that the pups are born at the same time every year. Nine months later – roughly the same gestation period as human beings – the pup is born. Soon afterwards, the adults mate again, and the whole cycle repeats itself.

Common seal pups can swim almost as soon as they are born, which means that – unlike grey seals – the female common seal is able to feed while suckling her young. She does not have to remain on land until her offspring is weaned, which happens about a month after it is born. Another difference between the two species is that the common seal pup is dark in colour, whereas the grey seal pup has a white coat.

This species is found mostly around the coasts of Scotland and eastern England, and common seals are generally scarce or absent in the south and

Common seal pups are usually born during the summer months, giving them plenty of time to grow and mature before the bad weather of autumn and winter sets in.

west. Common seals are also known as harbour seals, which is a more appropriate name because they tend to spend more time closer to the shore than their larger relative. They prefer to live in estuaries and along rocky shorelines, where they often haul themselves out of the water to rest on sandbanks for long periods at a time. These seals are wonderfully adapted to oceanic life, with a thick layer of blubber beneath their skin to keep them warm even when waters are icy cold; sensitive whiskers so that they can detect shoals of fish; and the ability to stay underwater – at depths of up to 200 metres – for at least 20 minutes at a time, and often far longer.

They also often appear in rivers, sometimes quite a way upstream, where they may be momentarily mistaken for an otter because they are on the small side for a seal, reaching a length of about 1.5 metres and weighing about 130 kilograms. Females tend to outlive the males, reaching an age of up to 35 years compared with just 20–25 years for the male.

Like all seals, they often come into conflict with fishermen, as they take many of the same fish that they are after, including mackerel, herring and cod.

Common seals may be inelegant on land, but beneath the waves they reveal a grace, beauty and ability to swim at speed to hunt down their fishy prey.

Riots at the roadside

During the months of June, July and August, in town and country, the hard grey tarmac of our open roads is softened by a riot of colour spilling over from the adjoining banks and verges. Myriad wild flowers come into bloom, in turn attracting insects such as beetles, hoverflies and bumblebees, ensuring that, up and down the country, from motorway verges to the sides of country lanes, our summer flora shows itself at its very best.

Of all our native roadside plants, surely the most widespread and familiar is the tall, creamy-white umbellifer known by more than 50 local folk-names, but generally called cow parsley or, more romantically, Queen Anne's lace. (This eponym was given because Queen Anne would often tour her realm during the plant's peak flowering season, and as she saw the flowers out of her carriage window she assumed that her subjects had strewn the roadsides with lace to welcome her.) The plant also has other, less pretty, names including adder's meat, dog parsley, rabbit's meat, whiteweed and the more sinister devil's parsley – probably a result of confusing this plant with the larger, poisonous hogweed.

Appearing as if by magic in late spring and early summer, cow parsley turns roadside verges white in just a few days. But as the summer progresses, it must compete with other, more striking plants, including two imports from abroad.

Rosebay willowherb appears from June onwards, in vibrant patches of reddish-purple. An accidental import from North America, this plant chooses to grow on recently disturbed soil, and like other imported plants, including Oxford ragwort, it has spread rapidly around the country by virtue of its tiny seeds being swept along in the slipstream of passing cars.

Another plant of similar hue is the red valerian, which was probably brought here accidentally by sailors from the Mediterranean in the Tudor era, so it is now very well established as a 'wild flower', especially in the south and west of the country. Its deep reddish-mauve flowers are a familiar sight along roadside verges in early to midsummer.

As the season progresses, the cow parsley's larger relative, hogweed, comes into bloom. Hogweed is equally good for feeding insects, which cling to the tiny flower heads in order to suck at the nectar. Along roadsides and in adjacent fields other summer plants begin to appear: purple thistles, deep brown docks and scarlet poppies. Our largest native daisy, the magnificent ox-eye daisy, may be in bloom alongside these plants all season long.

Every one of these roadside plants provides plenty of nectar for insects as they bloom, and then later in the season they offer valuable food for birds, too, such as finches, sparrows and buntings, in the form of their seeds.

Up and down the country, from motorway verges to the sides of country lanes, our summer flora shows itself at its very best.

Roadside verges often have a better display of wild flowers than farmed fields, as they are generally free from being sprayed with herbicides.

Meadows through the seasons

A meadow in bloom is a quintessentially British sight, and a real indicator of summer, but it is a landscape which takes on many other beautiful faces through the changing seasons. In spring the grasses are punctuated with fritillaries and other bulbs, in summer the swards experience an invasion of colour, and as autumn turns to winter the desiccated seedheads are rimed with frost. As well as being aesthetically pleasing, of course, meadows provide an invaluable source of food and shelter for a multitude of small mammals, insects and birds.

Lady of the lamp

On a warm, muggy summer's night, when clouds obscure the light of the moon, a strange phenomenon occurs. As the last glimmer of dusk fades away to the west, and darkness descends, so a bright pinprick of luminous green light appears; followed by another, and another, until the ground at the base of hedgerows is lit up like an unseasonal Christmas display.

This is the glow worm; a tiny, otherwise insignificant little creature, just 15 millimetres long, but with an extraordinary ability to create light in the darkness. It is not in fact a worm, but a small beetle, one of many in the family Lampyridae, commonly known as fireflies.

The bright glow is made only by the wingless female, and comes from the last few segments of her abdomen. This is a rare example amongst terrestrial creatures of a phenomenon known as 'bioluminescence' – the ability of living organisms to generate light. She emits this light to find a partner: the males, who are smaller and able to fly, pass overhead and as they do so are attracted by the glow, so they descend to mate. Nothing is left to chance by the female, for on a dark, moonless night the glow can be seen up to 50 metres away from its source.

Scientists have studied the glow worm to try to discover how she can be so energy-efficient: almost 100 per cent of her energy is turned into light, a percentage far greater than that of any manmade bulb. The light creates virtually no heat energy; it is made using a substance called luciferin, which reacts with oxygen in the air to produce the insect's eerie glow. The light has another useful purpose: just like other insects, which use bright colours to warn predators not to eat them, it indicates that the glow worm tastes unpleasant.

Her moment of glory is brief, though, for after a few weeks of glowing she mates, lays her eggs, turns off her light and dies. Her larvae, however, are fearsome predators, hunting down slugs and snails to devour.

Glow worms are fairly widespread in Britain; they are found in southern England, the Midlands, Wales and parts of lowland Scotland. Although they can be spotted from May through to late August and early September, their peak season is June and July, the period when the females are glowing.

Unfortunately, however, numbers of glow worm have plummeted in recent years: partly due to the spraying and cutting of roadside verges, but mainly because of light pollution coming from our homes, factories, street lights and motor vehicles. These powerful alternative sources of light confuse the males, so they often fail to find the female's much tinier glow. A campaign to reduce light pollution, especially in the countryside, may be this little beetle's only hope of survival.

The female glow worm emits her extraordinarily bright green light on warm, muggy evenings during the summer months.

ANTS

Of the 36 species of ant that live in the British Isles, the wood ant is the largest, measuring 8–10mm long. As its name suggests, they are mostly to be found in woodland environments, living in colonies. They are energetic workers, building large nests on the woodland floor using dead leaves, pine needles and small twigs that they gather and weave together to make a mound. While some of the ants stay at home and look after the young of the colony, others go out to hunt and scavenge for food. Wood ants are able to defend themselves on these trips because they produce formic acid in glands at the tip of their abdomen (hence their species name, *Formica rufa*) which they will spray at predators and also prey. They have even been known to spray at unsuspecting humans! This acid can be beneficial to other wildlife, though, and many birds, such as jays, will provoke ants to spray acid onto their feathers to kill off any lurking feather lice and other parasites.

Singing for survival

On a warm summer's day, one bird above all others provides the soundtrack across the whole of rural Britain. From the arable farms of East Anglia to the sheep pastures of the Yorkshire Dales, from the London parks to the grouse moors of Scotland, and from the Isles of Scilly to Shetland (1,000 miles to the north), the skylark is in song.

   What is it about this little brown bird that excites so much joy from those who hear it? First, there is the song: a tumultuous outpouring of notes, rising and falling in pitch, and so scrambled together that you begin to think the bird might not be able to keep up with itself. Then there is the means by which this extraordinary song is delivered: so high in the sky that the bird is often virtually

out of sight. Even if you can spot it, it appears to be little more than a speck, as if a fly is hovering high in the sky.

Then there is the skylark's sheer persistence. It can sometimes seem as if it is singing throughout the daylight hours, so constant is the sound; though in fact this misconception arises from the presence of several males, each of their songs overlapping.

No wonder that the skylark has such an important place in the pantheon of British birds. For centuries, poets and musicians have celebrated its sound, most famously in two nineteenth-century poems, Shelley's 'Ode to a Skylark', written in 1820, and George Meredith's 'The Lark Ascending', written in the Victorian era; and also in Ralph Vaughan Williams's musical piece of the same name, which took its inspiration from Meredith's poem. But ironically for what seems such a quintessentially English poem, Shelley's ode was inspired by a country walk with his sister, Mary Shelley, while they were in Italy!

So what of the skylark itself? It is a smallish, brown bird – a little bigger than a sparrow, with streaked brown plumage and a distinctive crest. Skylarks nest on the ground, where their eggs and chicks are very vulnerable to predators. To combat this, they have evolved the precautionary strategy of landing some distance from the actual nest site, and then approaching it on the ground, where they are less likely to be followed by any bird of prey or mammal wanting an easy meal.

Skylarks are highly adaptable birds and can be found in a very wide range of habitats, from arable farmland, heathland and moorland to city parks and offshore islands – indeed anywhere with the combination of long grass (for nesting) and a supply of insect food for their chicks. As a result, in the late 1960s and early 1970s the skylark was recorded as the most widely distributed of all British birds.

But sadly, in recent years the skylark has declined in both range and numbers – down more than 70 per cent in the past 25 years, and is now scarce or absent from many of its former haunts. This is almost entirely down to the post-war rise of industrial farming, in which the need to increase yields means that the features that make a habitat suitable for skylarks – a mosaic of different microhabitats, providing places for them to feed and breed – have been systematically removed.

Conservationists have, in cooperation with farmers, managed to restore the bird's habitat by creating 'skylark patches', where skylarks can find a place to nest and food for their chicks; and by allowing some fields to return to stubble in winter, providing vital seeds at this lean time of year. It remains to be seen whether this is a case of too little, too late. In the meantime we can still enjoy the song of the skylark on a fine summer's day – but for how much longer?

No other bird sings quite as high in the sky, or for quite as long, as the skylark – the subject of many a poetic or musical tribute.

Natural born killers

One group of mammals, known as the mustelids, are sleek, efficient predators that are able to attack and kill animals much larger than themselves. As well as the otter and badger, which we have discussed earlier, this group includes four elusive creatures that are rarely seen but nevertheless have an important impact on wildlife and ecosystems all over Britain.

Summer is an easy time for these efficient killers, as there is plenty of food available in the form of rabbits, small mammals and ground-nesting birds, on which they are able to feed both themselves and their young.

The two most familiar mustelids, the stoat and the weasel, are often confused with one another, partly because their biggest difference – their relative size – is hard to judge when viewing a lone animal. They are both long and slender, with a chestnut-brown head and upperparts and creamy yellow underparts. Both have a long tail, but crucially the stoat's tail is tipped with black, which is a useful way to tell it apart from its smaller relative. Both run very fast, but being curious creatures they will sometimes stop and stand up on their hind legs like a meerkat to look around them, before dashing away into dense cover, out of sight.

The weasel is the world's smallest carnivorous mammal, reaching a length of about 20–25 centimetres plus 10–12 centimetres of tail, but owing to its slim build it weighs just 50–100 grams. Despite its tiny size, the weasel punches well above its weight, being able to attack and kill mice and voles, and also baby rabbits, which weigh considerably more than it does.

The weasel has to be a ruthless predator, as it must eat one-third of its body weight every single day just to stay alive. So it is very active, hunting along hedgerows and stone walls in order to pursue or ambush its prey, and also heading underground through tunnels and holes.

The larger stoat is a highly efficient killer, mainly preying on rabbits, which it despatches with a bite to the neck. In spring and summer stoats vary their diet by taking the eggs and chicks of ground-nesting birds and the occasional insect.

Both weasels and stoats mate during the early part of summer and give birth the following spring. The stoat generally has just one litter, of up to 12 kits, while the weasel has four or five offspring, but it may have a second litter in July or August if there is enough food available. Like most small- to medium-sized mammals, the young grow incredibly quickly: they are weaned after a few weeks and can be off hunting their own prey and even breeding after just a few months.

Both stoats and weasels are widely distributed across virtually the whole of Britain, apart from a few offshore islands, though like other creatures that failed

A family of stoats, the youngsters ready to learn from their parents how to be a ruthless predator.

to cross the land bridge between our two countries before the Irish Sea was formed, the weasel is absent from Ireland. In contrast the two larger mustelids, the pine marten and polecat, have a much more restricted range. Polecats are mainly found in Wales and the border counties between England and Wales, with a small population in western Scotland. Pine martens have a much more northerly distribution, in the northern and western highlands of Scotland and parts of Ireland, where they generally live in dense forests.

These two species are, like stoats and weasels, predominantly nocturnal, though the long hours of daylight during the summer months mean that they also frequently emerge around dawn and dusk. And they also share the same instinct as stoats and weasels in that they are opportunistic hunters, feeding on everything from small mammals and birds, through eggs, insects and berries to carrion.

Like most British mammals, pine martens and polecats give birth in late spring and early summer, to coincide with the greatest availability of food for both the young and their busy parents. While polecats can have a litter of as many as ten kits, pine martens have much smaller families, with just two young. Young polecats are tiny – weighing just 10 grams at birth – and are covered with a layer of silky white hair which turns brown after three or four weeks. They usually appear in the open with their mothers at two or three months old, in June or July.

Sightings at sea

As summer nears its zenith, sightings of another group of mammals reach their peak. Cetaceans – the mighty whales, and the smaller but equally charismatic dolphins and porpoises – occur in surprisingly large numbers off Britain's coasts, and although many stay far out to sea, others can be seen from the shore.

The best-known resident cetacean in British waters is the bottlenose dolphin. There are two main populations: one in the waters east of Inverness, in the Moray Firth; and the other in Cardigan Bay, in the Irish Sea off the west coast of Wales. Both these areas have become well-known hotspots for 'dolphin tourism', as enthusiasts gather on coastal headlands to watch these creatures, or head out on specially organised boat trips.

Unfortunately for dolphin enthusiasts – and for the dolphins themselves – this rise in interest has been paralleled by a decline in dolphin numbers; or at least in the number of sightings. This may be to do with the perennial problems of marine pollution and disturbance from shipping traffic, but there are also more worrying threats, including the reduction of their food supply through overfishing, and the effects of climate change.

The apparent increase in unexplained beachings of pods of dolphins, during which many of the animals become stranded and die, has been put down to the effects of military sonar, which may be interfering with the dolphins' sophisticated internal navigation system.

Dolphins have a very high place in our affections: partly because of their undoubted intelligence, including the ability to communicate with one another through a form of language, and also because they appear to be smiling at us! In fact they can be as vicious as any creature: scientists studying dolphins often identify them by the markings they have acquired during fights.

Other cetaceans seen regularly off our coasts include the smaller harbour porpoise and the larger minke whale. Porpoises are less sociable and more solitary than dolphins, and are often seen fairly close to shore. They can be identified by their smaller size and short, triangular dorsal fin, superficially like that of a shark. Minke whales are mainly found off the coast of northwest Scotland, especially around the Western Isles, where they follow flocks of seabirds in order to find food.

In recent years, climate change appears to have prompted several other species of whale to venture northwards from their usual home in the Bay of Biscay off the coast of France and Spain, into the waters off southwest England and the Irish Sea. At times these have included some of the biggest creatures on the planet, including the mighty fin whale.

In the past, the fin whale – second only to the blue whale as the largest creature ever – was a scarce and irregular visitor off the UK, with perhaps only one or two sightings a year. So recent gatherings of more than 20 fin whales feeding as close as 80–100 kilometres offshore, between the Cornish coast and southwest Wales, are unprecedented. It is thought that the fin whales may have been following vast flocks of krill – their main source of food – which have in turn moved north as sea waters warm up.

As climate change continues to affect sea temperatures, the good news for us is that scientists predict that sightings of other rare whales – perhaps even the mighty blue whale, currently a very rare and occasional visitor to our offshore waters – will increase.

Bottlenose dolphins are an increasingly common sight off the coasts of west Wales and Scotland, performing their acrobatic leaps close to the shore.

The essence of summer

Dragonflies are amongst our largest, most spectacular and most fascinating insects. They can fly at a top speed of over 20 miles per hour and are so manoeuvrable that they can stop, turn, and change direction in an instant, thanks to their complex arrangement of four wings, each parallel to the body and powered by huge flight muscles.

Dragonflies have been described as 'the essence of summer', and few other creatures are so closely linked with our warmest and sunniest season. Although the earliest species, the hairy dragonfly, usually appears by late April or early May, and the last, the common darter, may be on the wing well into November, the peak season for these showy insects is the two main summer months of July and August, when most are on the wing.

Britain has fewer than 25 regularly occurring species of dragonfly, out of a world total of more than 2,700 species. But what we lack in variety we make up for in numbers. On a sunny day in midsummer a wetland such as the Norfolk Broads may be home to thousands of these insects, cruising up and down as they search for smaller creatures on which to prey, or perching on the stem of a reed or other aquatic plant.

One of the commonest and most obvious dragonflies at this time of year is the huge and impressive emperor, which at 10 centimetres long is one of Britain's largest insects. Males are azure blue in colour, with a green head and thorax and a black line running along the top of the abdomen; females are a greener shade. The emperor is usually on the wing from late June into August, while its close relatives the southern and brown hawkers (the latter the only common dragonfly with yellowish-brown, as opposed to transparent, wings) generally appear slightly later, from late July into August and September.

Other familiar groups of dragonflies include the chasers: with distinctive chunky bodies and a useful habit of perching still for long periods, enabling close approach; the skimmers, with longer, slimmer bodies and a habit of perching on the ground; and the darters, smaller insects with slender bodies.

Some species of dragonfly have adapted to specific habitats or geographical areas. So the common hawker (which despite its name is quite restricted in range) and the golden-ringed dragonfly (a huge black-and-yellow insect like a giant, elongated wasp) both prefer acid streams, and so are mainly found in moorland and heathland habitats, with their acidic soils, in the north and west of Britain.

In the far north, Scottish specialities include several species that have adapted to the cooler conditions of the Highlands, where they can take advantage of the very long summer days to hunt for food. These include the

Dragonflies have been described as 'the essence of summer', and few other creatures are so closely linked with our warmest and sunniest season.

The male black darter is the only black British dragonfly. It is a small species which makes its home on heaths and moors, particularly in the north of the country.

A hard harvest

As July gives way to August, and crop farmers all over Britain begin to gather their crops, spare a thought for Britain's smallest – and arguably most endearing – rodent, the harvest mouse, whose nest falls victim to the combine harvester.

The harvest mouse is minuscule: weighing five grams and measuring eight centimetres long, it is dwarfed by other mice and voles. Only the pygmy shrew, our smallest mammal and an insectivore rather than a rodent, is tinier. The name is something of a misnomer; for although these creatures do often live in fields of crops such as wheat or oats, they are equally at home in long grass and hedgerows, and even live in reedbeds. In all these varied habitats they use their prehensile tail – a feature unique amongst Old World mammals – to grip tightly onto vegetation as they move around in this primarily vertical habitat. Their feet are also adapted to cling onto stems, being broad and with an opposable toe that enables a more effective grip. Its long, hairless tail, along with its small size, yellowish-brown coat and white underparts, mean it is easy to identify.

With a lifespan of just 18 months (unless brought to an abrupt end by a predator), harvest mice must – like other small mammals – reproduce as soon as they can in order to pass on their genes. To do so they build an extraordinary nest, anytime during the period from May through to October, weaving grass stems around tall vegetation to form a ball about 10 centimetres in diameter, in which there may be as many as eight tiny young. Like most small mammals, harvest mice can breed at an early age, and they will bear up to three litters in a single breeding season. The peak time for breeding is in late summer: during August and September, when three-quarters of all litters are born.

Harvest mice feed mainly on seeds, though they also eat plenty of small insects in summer; and like many rodents they switch their diet in autumn to feed on fruits and berries, in order to build up enough energy to survive the cold winter months. They do not hibernate (of Britain's rodents, only the dormouse does so) but they do hide away, often burrowing beneath the soil to keep warm.

Harvest mice are mainly found in southern Britain, though a few can be found right up to the Scottish borders. However, like so many farmland creatures, numbers of these mice have declined steadily since the Second World War. Today's industrial-scale farming methods, with the widespread removal of hedgerows and use of combine harvesters, have together reduced the population of this tiny rodent, although conservationists are now working closely with farmers to help save this iconic creature of the British countryside.

The harvest mouse is Britain's smallest rodent, and clings onto stems of grass and reeds with its prehensile tail.

Midsummer moult

As summer reaches its peak in July and early August, a strange phenomenon occurs amongst Britain's duck population. Almost overnight, the brightly coloured males seem to vanish, leaving a motley collection of tatty brown creatures behind.

In fact the males have not disappeared but have simply begun their annual moult, in which they lose their splendid breeding plumage and closely resemble the drabber females – a state known as 'eclipse' plumage.

Both males and females moult at this time of year because after the efforts of raising a family of ducklings, their feathers have become worn and tatty; and if they remained in that condition they would have problems surviving

the coming autumn and winter. So they undergo the complex process of moult, in which new, bright feathers gradually replace the old ones. They do this at this time of year because it is a period when food is plentiful, and the vegetation around the edge of lakes, pools and rivers is at its fullest. This enables them to hide away from predators such as foxes or stoats, which find the ducks easier to catch when moulting because they are less able to escape due to the poor quality of their flight feathers.

The process of acquiring a whole new set of feathers can take time – at least two or three months, although this varies between species. Mallards – our most widespread and easily most familiar duck – generally begin the process of moulting in July and are in their spanking new plumage by September or October. The contrast between the blackish-brown eclipse garb and the bottle-green head and magenta breast of the new plumage is extraordinary.

> As summer reaches its peak ... ducks undergo the complex process of moult, in which new, bright feathers gradually replace the old ones.

Most birds choose to moult at this time of year for the same reasons – small birds in particular can hide away in the forest canopy, staying still and silent so that it can seem as if there are absolutely no birds present. Juvenile birds – those born earlier in the year – also moult now. Some species acquire adult plumage straightaway, while others, such as the gulls, acquire what is known as 'first-winter' plumage, followed later by 'first-summer' and 'second-winter', as it can take up to four years for them to become fully adult.

Migrant songbirds such as warblers and flycatchers have an even more important reason to acquire new feathers in late summer, as they will soon have to fly thousands of miles and cannot afford to be in anything other than tip-top condition. Some songbirds also moult again, in late winter or early spring, in time for the breeding season ahead, when their bright, clean plumage will help them attract a mate.

One group of birds, the raptors – day-flying birds of prey such as buzzards, hawks and eagles – moult in a different way. Because they cannot afford to lose the power of flight, as they must hunt or scavenge for food each day, they replace one or two feathers at a time, so that gaps appear in their broad wings where a feather is missing and waiting to be replaced.

By the time autumn arrives, most birds will have moulted into the plumage in which they will spend the winter – and on ponds up and down the country, the vanishing male ducks will have reappeared in all their splendour.

This mallard is keeping its feathers in tip-top condition by preening them with its bill.

The great winter getaway

As the summer sunshine brings warmth and plenty to the land, it is easy to imagine that the season will last forever. But our wild creatures are already readying themselves for autumn, and one group of organisms is preparing for the biggest mass movement on the planet: the autumn migration of birds.

The vast majority of migrants are small, insect-eating songbirds; those that would struggle to find enough insects to keep up their weight, and energy levels, during a cold winter. Birds that feed on flying insects, such as swallows, martins and swifts, have no option – there are virtually no flying insects available from October to March. But those that forage for insects amongst the foliage of trees and bushes fall into two categories: those that migrate and those that stay at home. Some, such as warblers, flycatchers and chats, migrate; either all the way to sub-Saharan Africa; or simply as far as Spain, Portugal or North Africa.

Yet many insect-eating species do stay put in Britain. Treecreepers and goldcrests, for example, forage for tiny insects and grubs in the bark of trees or amidst the foliage of conifers; while blue tits switch their diet and feed mainly on seeds and nuts – including, of course, those provided by us in our gardens.

For those that do migrate, and especially species that are true long-distance migrants – heading to West Africa, or even all the way across the Equator to southern Africa – the timing of their departure is critical. In part this is triggered, as it was in the spring, by changes in day length on either side of the autumn equinox. But local weather plays a part too: if autumn comes early, in the first weeks of September, many migrants will head off; although only once they have ensured they have put on enough extra weight in the form of fat reserves beneath their skin to sustain them. If, on the other hand, September stays warm and dry, they may linger, feeding on fruit and berries a little longer.

From late August onwards, swallows begin to gather on telegraph wires; chattering to one another, and from time to time swooping off as if rehearsing their departure. Many of these birds are juveniles – told apart from their parents by their shorter tails – and will be undertaking their very first journey south. Many, sadly, will not make it to their destination: blown off course by storms, killed by predators, or simply falling exhausted out of the sky.

But those that do make it reap the benefits of dividing their life between two homes: having enjoyed the long hours of daylight and abundant food of the northern summer, they steer clear of our winter and spend November to March amongst the big game on the African savannah, where insect food is abundant.

Knots gather in vast flocks at high tide, when they are forced off the mudflats and must wait until the waters fall again before they can feed.

Silken wings

On a fine early autumn morning, when a chill in the air offsets the warm sunshine for the first time in many months, we may witness one of the natural world's most extraordinary spectacles. For this is the time of year when baby spiders take to the air in vast, almost uncountable numbers, and embark on one of the most unpredictable of all nature's journeys.

Of course, baby spiders – also known as spiderlings – cannot fly, but needing to colonise new areas, they launch themselves into the atmosphere, at the mercy of wherever the autumn breezes carry them.

As the morning sun pokes above the horizon, each tiny spiderling starts to spin a long thread of fine, golden silk – one of the strongest-known materials, ounce for ounce. They wait until the wind begins to pick up, then piggyback the breeze to finally launch themselves into the air, using the thread – known as gossamer – to carry them aloft.

> On autumn mornings you may walk out to find the ground draped with thousands of discarded, delicate threads of spider's silk.

Most fall almost immediately to earth, unable to catch the breeze at exactly the right moment, but others may get their silk thread caught on bushes or branches and cannot get free. That is why, on autumn mornings, you may walk out to find the ground draped with thousands of discarded, delicate threads of spider's silk.

But those spiderlings that get the timing right, more by luck than by judgement, find themselves borne aloft – rather like bungee jumping in reverse – getting higher and higher until they rapidly go out of sight.

Incredibly, spiderlings have been found in the atmosphere at heights of almost 11,000 metres, which at almost seven miles above ground is higher than the summit of Mount Everest. Most, of course, fail to find any suitable habitat, but for those that do fall to Earth in the right place, where they can survive and prosper, the adventure was well worthwhile.

In autumn baby spiders launch themselves through the air between plants and other fixed structures, spinning a fine silken thread as they go.

Riders on the storm

Seabirds are amongst the most mysterious and enigmatic of all our wild creatures. Although they head onto the land to breed for a few months of the year, they spend the majority of their lives way out over the open ocean. Just occasionally, however, severe gales and storms in autumn or winter will bring them closer to shore; even, on rare occasions, right inland.

In these conditions, the passage of seabirds past coastal headlands can number in the thousands, as birds whose migratory journeys have been pushed off course by autumn gales try to reorient themselves and head back out to sea. Coastal headlands such as Flamborough Head in Yorkshire, St Ives in Cornwall, and the Butt of Lewis on the Outer Hebrides are well-known seabird hotspots; but when severe gales blow in from the Atlantic or the North Sea, almost any prominent headland may see a major passage of birds.

The commonest species are those that nest in our own seabird colonies: auks such as the guillemot, razorbill or puffin; gannets, Manx shearwaters, storm and Leach's petrels; and terns, kittiwakes and skuas. But other species come from much farther afield: great and sooty shearwaters breed in the distant south

Atlantic, on remote islands such as Tristan da Cunha, yet regularly pass our coasts every autumn on their usual migratory journeys, sometimes in considerable numbers.

Only when storms are exceptionally severe will some of these ocean-going birds become so disoriented that they fly inland, and end up on reservoirs, lakes and gravel-pits far from the sea. Leach's petrel – a small, dark seabird with a distinctive white rump – is especially prone to such wanderings; as is Sabine's gull, a delicate and beautiful creature which nests in the High Arctic and winters in the open ocean, and whose juvenile's zigzag wing pattern is similar to that of a commoner gull, the kittiwake. But even such powerful fliers as gannets can be swept inland, turning up in the most unlikely places.

Such unusual sightings may be only the tip of a much larger iceberg. Often, flocks of seabirds out at sea are hit by such a sudden storm that they either fall exhausted into the sea or, unable to fly against the wind, are swept onshore, where they tend to die. These incidents are, appropriately, known as 'wrecks', and may result in the deaths of many thousands of birds. Those that avoid being caught up in these incidents are fortunate, yet they will now have to survive in one of the world's most hostile environments – the open ocean – until they return again to their breeding grounds the following spring. For now, though, they will spend the entire winter at sea.

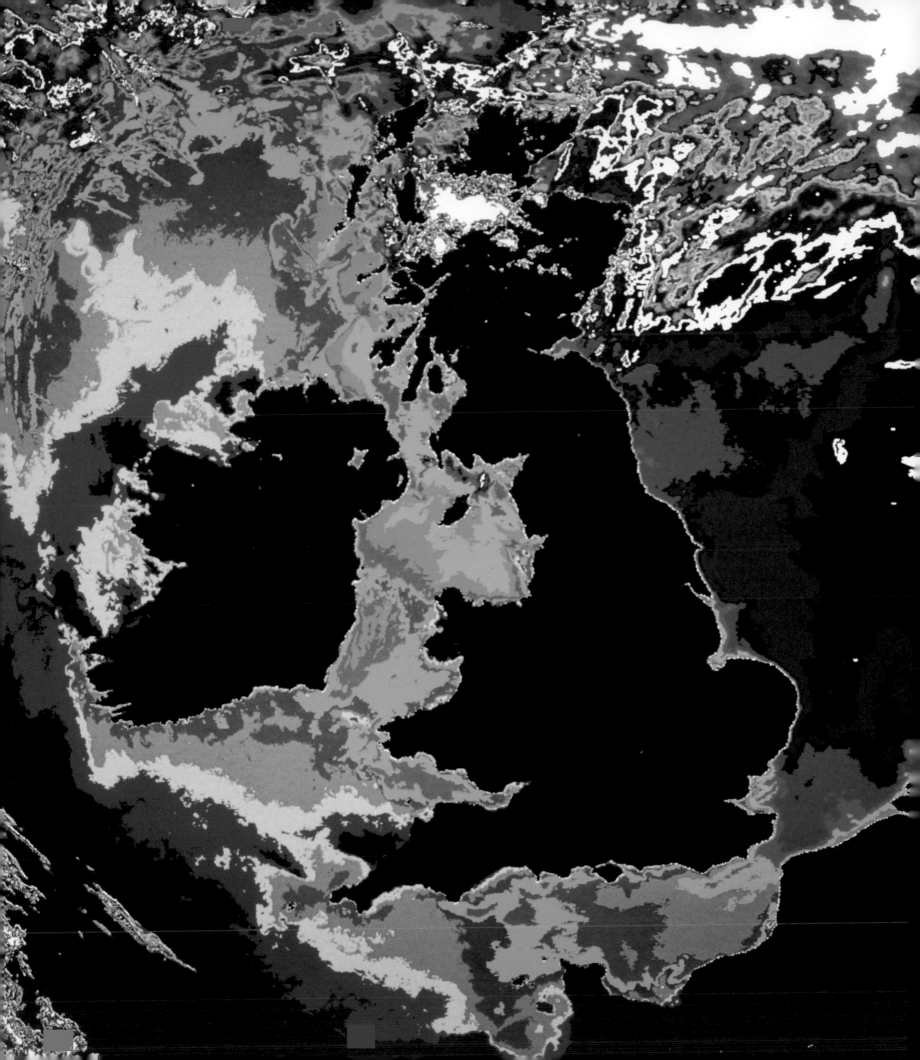

WATER TEMPERATURES AROUND BRITAIN

OPPOSITE: Sea surface temperatures around British Isles, shown from red (warmest), through yellow, green, then blue (coolest). Land masses shown as black (but black region in ocean at bottom left is an artefact). Cloud cover shown as white. Warmer seas to west of Britain caused by warm Gulf Stream current. Coastal waters appear warmer due to solar heating in the shallows.

Britain lies in the path of the North Atlantic Drift – the northern extension of the Gulf Stream. This ocean current originates in the Gulf of Mexico and carries warm water and air across the Atlantic to the shores of Northern Europe. The North Atlantic Drift is thought to contribute to keeping the temperatures in western and northern Europe far warmer than usual for this latitude. In Britain, the North Atlantic Drift particularly affects the southwest regions, with places such as Cornwall and the Scilly Isles enjoying an almost tropical climate in summer. The North Atlantic Drift also brings a wealth of wildlife to the shores of Britain – 'exotic' species such as sunfish, leatherback turtles and blue sharks (below) are known to visit during the summer months.

Mists and mellow fruitfulness

Late summer and early autumn see the high point of the fruiting season for many native and non-native plants. This is the time of year when apple orchards are reaching their peak; their fruit being harvested as eaters and cookers, while the bitter apples are taken off for use in cider-making.

Along our hedgerows and woodland edges, several common berry-bearing plants are laden with fruit at this time of year. Elder is one of the first to ripen: clusters of juicy, blackish-purple berries appearing from late August onwards. Elderberries are swiftly followed by those from two of our most familiar hedgerow plants: blackthorn and hawthorn.

Although in spring these two look fairly similar, their green foliage dotted with clumps of white blossom, by the autumn they appear very different from one another. The blackthorn produces deep purple fruit – sloes – that look like very small, hard plums and are bitter to the taste; these are famously used to make the traditional alcoholic beverage sloe gin. Hawthorn bushes produce vast numbers of red berries, whose brightly coloured clusters stud the green foliage.

Then there is the only one of these wild berries that we find palatable raw, the fruit of the bramble, known of course as the blackberry. These may appear as early as July, though the peak of the crop usually ripens in September.

All these berries are produced for a simple purpose: to envelop the seeds of these plants in a tasty, fleshy outer coating, so that birds and mammals will feed on them and transport the seeds elsewhere.

The by-product of this is that wild creatures have come to depend on the energy-giving fruit in order to build up fat reserves, either for migration or to survive the coming autumn and winter. Many small mammals, such as mice, voles and shrews, benefit from this high-energy food at this time of year, as do birds. Warblers such as the whitethroat and blackcap, about to embark on their journeys south to Africa, benefit hugely from this glut of food.

Later in the autumn, those fruits that remain – especially hawthorn berries – will attract another suite of migrant birds: thrushes such as the fieldfare and redwing from farther north and east, which arrive from mid-October onwards and throng the hedgerows throughout our countryside.

In autumn our hedgerows are rich in colour and fruit, providing a delicious banquet of berries for hungry birds and mammals.

AUTUMN
INTO
WINTER

As summer shifts into autumn, and the chill winds begin to blow, so wild animals prepare for the onset of the hardest season of all: winter. But even as migrant birds and insects head south, visitors arrive in Britain from the north. Squirrels, hedgehogs and dormice stock up on energy for the months ahead, while on misty mornings mushrooms miraculously appear in our woods and fields. As the year draws to a close, the cycle of nature reaches both an end and a new beginning as we and our wildlife await the New Year to come.

THE BEGINNING OF autumn is heralded, officially at least, with the arrival of the autumn equinox towards the end of September. Like the spring equinox six months earlier, this marks the point at which the Earth's axis is at 90 degrees to the Sun, and so the whole planet experiences 12 hours of daylight and 12 hours of darkness. From now on, the northern hemisphere begins to tilt away from the Sun and we enter the season of autumn; swiftly followed, in three months' time, by winter.

For the natural world, autumn is a time of preparation: for every creature to ensure that they are in the best possible place, and condition, to survive the rigours to come. For some – the migrant birds, butterflies and moths that visit us during the spring and summer months to breed – the reduction in the hours of daylight signals the time to depart, as they head south towards warmer climes. In this mass exodus, numbering millions of individuals, the swallows, swifts, cuckoos and warblers head all the way to Equatorial Africa.

But for the vast majority of animals, migration is simply not an option. They must either stay put in the place where they were born and raised, or they move a short distance to take advantage of a more equable environment where they have a better chance of surviving the winter.

So while the swallow embarks on its epic voyage to the southern tip of Africa – a journey of some 8,000 kilometres – and the red admirals and painted ladies head across the English Channel towards their ancestral home around the Mediterranean Sea, other birds such as the meadow pipit and skylark travel comparatively modest distances. They simply leave the moorland where they bred and come down towards the coasts, where the rigours of winter will be less pronounced, due to the warming influence of the sea.

For trees and other plants, which are, of course, literally rooted to the spot, the seasonal transformation that takes place at this time of year is arguably more profound than for those global voyagers, as they must undergo extraordinary changes to their metabolism in order to survive the long winter season. Thus the leaves of deciduous trees turn brown, and later drop to the ground, ensuring that trees do not waste energy and precious moisture; while flowering plants set seed and then, in the case of annuals, die, or for perennials, lie dormant until the following spring.

Mammals also spend this period of the year preparing for the coming winter, though they do so in different ways. Squirrels hoard food, for the autumnal glut of acorns and hazelnuts will not last, so they bury any surplus they gather. They rely on their extraordinary spatial memory to find these hidden food supplies again in a few months' time, when rediscovering their cache may mean the

difference between life and death. Those that they fail to find will eventually sprout, and may one day become full-grown trees – an ancient oak standing proud in the centre of a field may be the result of a squirrel's forgetfulness more than a thousand years ago.

In autumn, fruits and berries are plentiful along our hedgerows and roadside verges, as hawthorn and blackthorn, elder and bramble and – later in the season – holly, ivy and mistletoe produce their fleshy fruits to tempt any passing bird or mammal. These are a valuable lifeline for wildlife, as their energy content is high, enabling voles, dormice and small birds such as blackbirds and thrushes to accumulate fat reserves to keep them warm and healthy when the lean times come.

By the time Halloween gives way to the bonfires of 5 November, virtually all the summer visitors to our shores have departed, apart perhaps from the occasional straggler; a tardy swallow or house martin, searching in vain for the tiny insects it needs to embark on its southward journey. An Indian summer – an unexpected period of warm, sunny weather in mid-to-late autumn – may bring some solace. This usually sees the last gasp of the larger flying insects, as butterflies and dragonflies feed on the rotting flesh of windfall fruits, or bask in a sheltered, sunny spot in the corner of the garden.

But as well as being a period of death and departures, this is also a time for new arrivals, as millions of birds swarm into the country from the north and east to spend

the winter here. For ducks and geese, swans and waders, thrushes and starlings, Britain in autumn and winter is a land of opportunity, where our relatively mild temperatures (at least compared with places farther north and east) mean that food is surprisingly plentiful.

The first flurries of snow can bring surprising benefits. Scavengers such as foxes and buzzards profit from the rise in mortality of smaller creatures, while tiny voles make their burrows beneath the blanket of snow, safe in the knowledge that the kestrels and barn owls overhead cannot detect their presence.

All this change and activity happens over just three months. This is a period often dismissed by naturalists as the quietest time of year, but in fact it is actually one of great drama, even though many of these changes happen out of the sight of humans.

So as the winter solstice comes round once again, a few days before the Yuletide and New Year celebrations, we should not presume from the apparent lack of activity that nature has shut down altogether. On the contrary, the natural world is on the cusp of renewal: having done their best to survive the winter, Britain's plants and animals are already now preparing for the year ahead.

As the sun sets on 21 December, the shortest day, we know that from the following dawn the subsequent days will gradually lengthen; and the sights and sounds of nature will begin to build to a crescendo, as nature's cycle starts over once again.

Solitary slumber

It is often assumed that all or most of our small mammals hibernate over the winter months, but apart from bats, only two British mammals go into a state of true hibernation: the hedgehog and the common (or hazel) dormouse.

As its name – from the French word '*dormir*', meaning sleep – suggests, this endearing little mammal is known for its habit of sleeping. Indeed, no other British mammal sleeps for such a high proportion of the time: it is estimated that a typical dormouse is asleep for about two-thirds of its short life (dormice usually live for less than five years).

Like most small mammals, the main breeding period for dormice is during midsummer, when the female gives birth to a litter of four or five young. Born naked and blind, the young develop rapidly, their eyes open after 18 days and they are ready to leave the nest after one month. They need to be independent quickly, as from September they must prepare for their solitary winter sleep.

When awake, dormice are arboreal creatures, living almost entirely in the woodland canopy or along a hedgerow, sometimes many metres above the ground. They do so because they have a specialist diet: mainly feeding on the pollen and nectar from trees and shrubs, especially oak, sycamore, hawthorn and honeysuckle. They may also feed on insects, especially aphids, and as autumn approaches they feast on nuts and berries too, especially hazelnuts, sweet chestnuts and blackberries. These high-energy foods enable them to gain weight and build up reserves of fat prior to hibernation.

In October, a dormouse will descend to ground level, weaving a neat nest amongst the leaf litter on the forest floor or beneath a hedgerow. Once in its nest, its body temperature drops and its metabolism slows, so that it uses little energy.

It will remain asleep for up to seven months, emerging in May. During this time the dormouse goes through a cycle of deep and shallow sleep, rousing every week or so, but remaining inside the nest. Sadly, up to half of all hibernating dormice die because they have not built up sufficient fat reserves to keep them alive during hibernation. Unseasonably warm weather in winter is also a major killer, as it may prompt the dormouse to assume spring has come and so emerge too early. Even when it does emerge at the right time of year, cold wet weather can threaten the dormouse's chances of survival. However, it has a secret weapon to survive bad weather: by going into a brief state of torpor like full hibernation it can save energy until conditions are suitable for feeding again.

PREVIOUS PAGES: As winter draws in, Britain is visited by flocks of whooper swans arriving from the chillier climes of Iceland to sped the season here.

OPPOSITE: As its name suggests, the dormouse spends the majority of its life asleep, hibernating for up to seven months of every year.

Hidden hoards

For most British mammals, hibernation is not an option, as they have not evolved the ability to shut down their metabolism for the whole winter. Instead they must find enough food during the long winter months to survive until the following spring. Foraging is one way of doing this, but another method is to store food when it is plentiful, as an insurance policy against the lean times to come.

Our two species of squirrel – the native red and the introduced American grey – are experts at hiding food; and, more importantly, at being able to find it again. During the autumn, when hazelnuts and acorns are abundant, they are able to find enough food to get the energy they need; but if they relied on doing this during the winter, they would struggle to survive, especially during hard winters, when the ground may be covered for long periods in a thick layer of snow.

So once they have eaten their fill, squirrels will dig a small depression in the leaf litter beneath the trees – or, to the annoyance of gardeners, in flowerbeds and plant pots – and then pick up a nut and deposit it out of sight. Weeks or

The grey squirrel is the best known and one of the most widespread of all our non-native species, having been brought to Britain in the Victorian era from North America.

even months later, when food is scarce, they will search for the nut, find it, and feed.

Red and grey squirrels do this in different ways. The red squirrel puts all its eggs in one basket, creating a 'larder' in which it stores all its nuts. The advantage of this is that once it finds the cache, it can feed to its heart's content; but it also has two disadvantages. First, if the squirrel forgets where it has put the nuts all the effort it made during the autumn will have been wasted; second, if another animal stumbles across the hoard the squirrel risks losing it all.

Grey squirrels use a more scattergun technique, burying individual nuts in a range of places across a wide area. Their memory enables them to find many of the stored nuts, but a proportion always remains hidden – it is estimated that they find just over half. While searching for their many different caches, they may also stumble across the red squirrels' hoards. So where reds and greys are living alongside one another, the greys often get to the reds' food before they do. This is just one of the advantages that this invasive, alien species has over its native relative, which has enabled it to spread throughout much of Britain.

One unintended consequence of squirrels' occasional forgetfulness is that trees are able to spread more easily from these lost seeds, so that they colonise new areas and extend the forested area. Squirrels aren't the only wild creatures doing this, though: jays also hoard nuts and also sometimes forget where they are. But although they may have failed to discover their hidden hoard, in the longer term these animals are helping to replenish their forest habitat – which may not help *them*, but will benefit their descendants!

So how do squirrels and jays find any of their hidden caches of food, especially so long after hiding them? Like migrating birds, they appear to rely on a range of skills and techniques, including a spatial awareness of their territory, a memory for 'landmarks' such as a particular tree, and as they get closer to their hoard, using their acute sense of smell to home in on the exact spot. Red squirrels are also known to 'mark' their food before they hide it, using a scent gland in their cheek pouches.

In recent years, both red and grey squirrels have benefitted from our habit of feeding birds in our gardens, and in some cases, from householders putting up specially designed squirrel feeders to specifically help these animals. Squirrels are both ingenious and persistent, and have had their wits and agility tested using 'obstacle courses' designed by naturalists and wildlife filmmakers, in which the squirrel must overcome all sorts of physical and mental barriers before it can get to the food. But compared to having to remember where you hid a nut several months earlier, even these are child's play for a squirrel.

Today the red squirrel is confined mainly to northern England and Scotland, with isolated colonies in north Wales and on offshore islands in southern England.

Clever conifers

As September gives way to October and November, most trees take action to survive the coming winter by dropping their leaves. This has several benefits: as temperatures fall the trees are no longer able to photosynthesise and produce energy, so it makes sense to shed the leaves which would otherwise consume energy and provide nothing in return. This action also helps to prevent water loss by reducing the total surface area of the tree, and because the wind meets less resistance as it blows through bare branches, the tree is less likely to be blown over during autumn and winter gales and storms.

But some species of tree do not shed their leaves each autumn: the evergreens. These evergreens do lose their leaves, but they do so gradually and successively across the year so that they are always covered in foliage.

In tropical regions, many different kinds of tree and shrub are evergreen; but farther north most evergreens are conifers. Britain is home to just three native species of conifer: the mighty Scots pine, which once covered much of the Caledonian forest in the Scottish Highlands; the smaller juniper, which can be found on well-drained soils, especially limestone downlands and windswept moorlands; and the yew. As well as these few native conifers, Britain is home to many non-native species, including the familiar Norway spruce – otherwise known as the 'Christmas tree'. Others, including Douglas fir, were imported, often from former colonies of the British Empire by the plant hunters of the nineteenth century.

Conifers – whether native or not – are able to survive the rigours of the British winter because they have special adaptations to the conditions. These include thin waxy leaves (often known as 'needles') which greatly limit the amount of water loss by their reduced surface area. As a bonus, these leaves are generally inedible to the usual range of creatures that wreak such havoc on the leaves of deciduous trees, such as caterpillars, weevils and the larvae of beetles.

By shedding needles throughout the year to create a carpet of discarded needles on the ground beneath, pines and spruces also help to discourage the presence of competing deciduous trees, which are less suited to the acid soils the rotting needles help to create.

Conifers protect their seeds by surrounding them with a tough structure known as a cone, which opens when the seeds are ready to disperse – either by the cone simply falling off the tree, or by being dispersed by a bird such as crossbill which has adapted to obtain the seeds using its specially shaped bill. Once again, we see how different species adapt together over time to ensure their mutual survival.

PREVIOUS PAGES: When the autumn leaves begin to fall, hedgehogs and frogs forage for food in earnest to gain weight before they head into hibernation.

OPPOSITE: The mighty Scots pine is one of just three conifers native to Britain, and was once widespread throughout much of Scotland.

The waxwing is one of our most charismatic birds, whose unpredictable appearance in Britain only enhances its charm and beauty.

A waxwing winter

Rare birds usually turn up in remote places: offshore islands such as Fair Isle or Scilly, or coastal headlands including Dungeness, Portland Bill or Spurn Head. But one scarce species bucks the trend: the waxwing. More often than not, these stunning creatures are discovered in gardens, city streets or supermarket car parks, and not just as singles or in pairs but as whole flocks of them.

The reason for this is simple: waxwings feed on berries (just one bird can eat hundreds in a single day) and town planners and gardeners have done them a favour by planting a range of native and exotic berry-bearing plants, including cotoneaster, guelder rose and holly, in urban locations.

To see a flock of waxwings stripping a bush bare of its fruit is a truly wondrous sight. From a distance these plump, thrush-sized birds resemble starlings, but a closer look reveals their full beauty: warm brown plumage, with a splash of cinnamon beneath the tail; a perky, wispy crest; and most striking of all, the splash of yellow on the wings, tipped with red. It is this, so closely resembling the wax that was once used to seal letters, which gives the bird its unusual name. The call of the waxwing is also superficially similar to the sounds often made by starlings: a thin, metallic, high-pitched trill which penetrates the cold air.

Waxwings are only seen in Britain in autumn and winter; but unlike other songbirds that visit us at this time of year, such as the fieldfare and redwing, they are far from regular in their appearance. Indeed, along with a handful of other species, including the crossbill, they exhibit what is known as 'irruptive' behaviour. What this means is that during some years hardly any waxwings make the journey across the North Sea from their breeding grounds in Scandinavia and Arctic Russia, but in other years – usually about once a decade, and sometimes more frequently – they arrive here in tens of thousands.

This happens as a result of two factors: a boom in the numbers of birds following a successful breeding season, and a shortage of berries, which leave the waxwings with no choice but to head south and west to the British Isles in search of new supplies of food.

The first sign of a 'waxwing winter' usually comes along the east coasts of Scotland and England, where flocks may turn up any time from October onwards, lining up along telegraph wires in seaside resorts and coastal villages. They then begin to head inland, moving like an invading army, and gradually reaching the extreme southwest of Britain – sometimes even the Isles of Scilly.

As the winter goes on, and the berry crop diminishes, the flocks break up into ones and twos and the birds become harder to find. By March or early April, as winter draws to an end, they head back across the sea to Scandinavia, where they will breed again, to return to our shores again one day.

BATS

When insect numbers dwindle in late autumn, depriving bats of their essential source of sustenence, these mammals prepare for hibernation to survive the lean days of winter. Through summer and autumn bats feed voraciously to build up fat reserves, becoming increasingly torpid (sluggish and cold) when the weather is bad or their body temperature drops. As winter approaches, these periods of torpor last longer until eventually they enter into hibernation in quiet spaces such as disused buildings, trees or caves.

By February, the fat reserves that the bats built up over the previous summer and autumn are significantly reduced, meaning the bats must feed to survive. British bats feed primarily on insects, so they must time their emergence from hibernation to coincide with that of insects. On warm spring nights, bats may venture out in the hope of finding food and water. However, to fly the bats must bring their body temperature up from 10 degrees to 37 degrees, and to do this they must shiver for 20 minutes, which can use up the last of their precious resources. Just leaving the cave uses up the equivalent of 8 days' food reserves.

When conditions are good and insects are on the wing, bats are treated to a veritable feast, and even a tiny pipistrelle bat can eat up to 3,000 insects in one night. Such excesses help these mammals quickly regain condition after their winter fast, enabling them to put on the weight they will need for breeding.

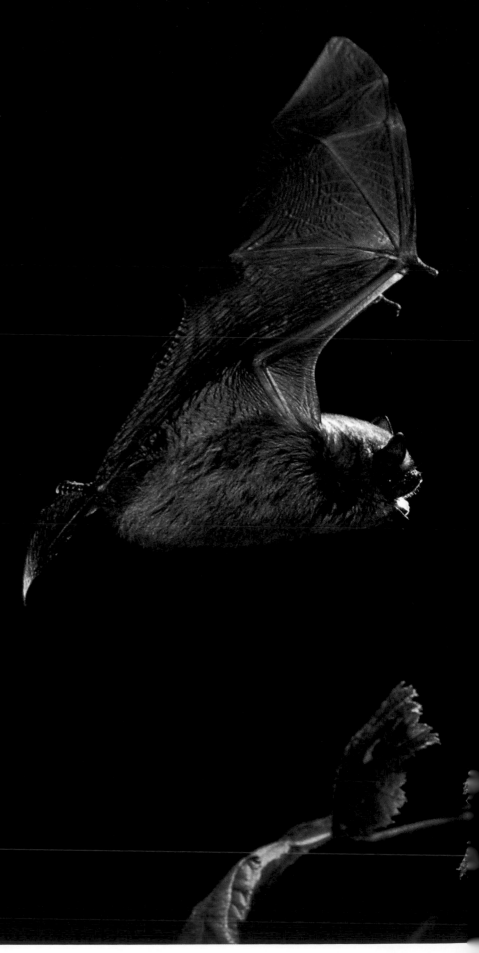

The Arctic arrivals

As the swallows and swifts, warblers and wheatears, cuckoos and corncrakes head south in their millions to spend the winter in Africa, the countryside seems bereft at their loss. But not for long: well before they return the following spring, millions more birds will arrive in Britain – coming here on migratory journeys just as eventful and potentially hazardous as those of the recently departed summer visitors.

Many of the autumn arrivals to our shores are waders – including the short-legged turnstone, the grey-and-white sanderling, and the larger, plumper knot – which breed on the Arctic tundra. There they can take advantage of virtually 24 hours of daylight in high summer, and a plentiful supply of insects.

As autumn approaches these birds head south, gathering around our shorelines and estuaries, each choosing an aspect of the coast that suits them best. Thus turnstones gather in small flocks on rocky shores, where their mottled winter plumage enables them to blend into the background. Sometimes they are joined by a scarcer wader, the purple sandpiper, which despite its colourful name is a dark grey shade during the autumn and winter months.

Sanderlings are much easier to see, as they tend to stay along the shoreline, running along on their tiny black legs like clockwork mice as the waves lap around their feet, and digging their short bills into the sand to obtain what morsels of food they can find.

The knot usually gathers in much bigger flocks, especially at high tide, when the birds are forced off the mudflats as the sea rises, and take refuge in huge roosts on nearby land. They huddle together for warmth and safety, grabbing fitful sleep as they wait nervously for the tide to drop once again so they can resume feeding.

Other common wintering waders include dunlin, redshank, grey and golden plovers and curlew, each of which has a different feeding technique, dictated by the shape and size of their bills. So while the plovers use their short, stubby bills to pick food off the surface of the mud or sand, dunlin, redshank and curlew probe theirs beneath the surface to find food, the curlew using its long, downcurved bill to go deeper than any other feeding wader.

The other main category of wintering birds is wildfowl – ducks, geese and swans – that come here from many different points of the compass, ranging from the northwest and north all the way round to the east. Pale-bellied Brent geese come from eastern Canada and Greenland; pink-footed geese and whooper swans from Iceland; barnacle geese from Spitsbergen; and Bewick's swans and white-fronted geese from Siberia.

Turnstones often gather on rocky shores, harboursides and even on boats, belying their origins in the High Arctic.

A secure future for our seals

As autumn gales begin to blow and the temperature drops, most British mammals have already come to the end of the breeding season. But one – the grey seal – is about to enter the most crucial part of its annual lifecycle, as the females prepare to give birth.

Sometime between late September and December, female grey seals haul themselves out onto beaches, mostly at traditional colonies where they feel safe, such as the Monach Isles off the northwest coast of Scotland, the Farne Islands off Northumberland, Donna Nook in Lincolnshire, and Blakeney Point in North Norfolk. Each female will give birth to a single pup, usually weighing

about 14–15 kilograms and covered in white fur, which is thought to be a legacy from the last Ice Age when this would enable the pup to be camouflaged amongst the ice and snow.

Soon after being born, the pup begins to suckle. For the following two to three weeks it will feed voraciously on the mother's milk, which being very rich in both fat and protein enables the young seal to more than double its weight in a very short period. Having moulted its white fur and adopted the adult's mottled, grey-brown coloration, the pup is then abandoned by its mother at about three weeks old. It usually remains on the beach for a few days until it is finally driven into the sea by hunger.

Meanwhile, the male grey seals have been competing with one another for the right to mate, in fierce, prolonged, and often bloody contests. Now the exhausted and hungry female, who has not fed at all while suckling her pup and has been surviving on her fat reserves, must submit to the winning male. After mating she delays implanting the fertilised egg into her womb for three months, so that she always gives birth at the same time every year.

Grey seals are one of two species of seal found off our coasts, the other being the smaller common, or harbour, seal. Weighing up to 440 kilograms, the grey seal is Britain's largest regular breeding mammal – its closest rival, the red deer, is only half its weight.

About 200,000 grey seals live around our shores, which at almost half the world population makes the UK globally important for this species. The importance of the grey seal population in the UK has been recognised for almost a century: the Grey Seals Protection Act of 1914, passed after they had been hunted almost to extinction, made this the first species to be legally protected anywhere in the world.

Their recent increase in numbers has not made them popular with fishermen, however, who complain of declining fish stocks and damaged nets. On the other side of the coin, a rise in 'seal tourism' is bringing much-needed income to coastal economies around Britain's shores. As with many of our wild creatures, the future of the grey seal depends on finding a balance between the many competing interests surrounding it.

Against the current

Of all Britain's wild creatures, the salmon, rightly known as 'the king of fish', makes one of the most incredible journeys. The Atlantic salmon's sheer power, strength and determination are truly incredible, especially in autumn, when it undergoes one of the most strenuous and difficult tests faced by any living creature.

Salmon are unusual amongst fish in that they have evolved a dual lifecycle: spending part of their lives in freshwater rivers and part out at sea, in a saltwater environment. Their life begins upstream, in clear, unpolluted rivers. The vast majority of the thousands of eggs produced by a single salmon never hatch at all, having been eaten by a wide range of river creatures, including amphibians, ducks and other species of fish.

Even when the young salmon do hatch, and begin to feed and grow, their chances of survival are minuscule. But those that do manage to survive eventually swim downstream, all the way out to sea, where they change colour from red to silver and adapt to living and feeding in salt water.

Six years later, they finally mature, and during autumn they begin the long haul back upriver to the same place where they were born. Here, the problems really begin: most salmon rivers are fast-flowing, as salmon need well-oxygenated water to find food. This means that to swim upstream the salmon not only have to fight against the rapid current, but must also scale obstacles such as rocky gorges and waterfalls.

They do so by using their extraordinary muscles to leap right out of the water and over any barriers in their way, sometimes scaling obstacles more than three and a half metres high: the equivalent of a human being leaping over a two-storey building.

Most perish, exhausted, along the way, or fall victim to anglers, or to natural predators including otters, herons and sea eagles. But for the few that do make it back home, the rewards are potentially great. They mate, and as the exhausted male swims off to die, the female makes one last effort, producing up to 7,000 eggs, before she too perishes.

With such a varied suite of ecological requirements, and such a challenging lifecycle, salmon are very vulnerable to environmental change. In the decades after the Second World War, pollution was the main threat to their survival, as tons of sewage, farm chemicals and industrial waste were poured into our river systems. Following the cleaning up of our rivers, the salmon made a good recovery, returning to many of their former haunts in major rivers such as the Tyne, Tees and Thames.

Atlantic salmon make the most extraordinary journey upstream to their breeding grounds, where they mate, lay their eggs and then die, exhausted.

But in recent years new factors have begun to threaten the species. Salmon farming has become established on an industrial scale around the coasts of Scotland, and there are now more than 50 farmed salmon for every one in the wild. Farmed salmon are kept in such cramped, sedentary conditions that they become susceptible to parasitic lice, which can transfer to wild fish and reduce their lifespan; as a result of this and the impacts of climate change when they are out at sea, the number of salmon returning to our rivers to spawn has been dramatically reduced.

Help is, fortunately, at hand: salmon rivers are being restocked with fish raised in captivity, while 'salmon ladders' are being installed on many rivers to enable the fish to climb waterfalls and other obstacles more easily. But as every autumn sees a fall in the numbers of salmon returning to their birthplace, the sight of salmon leaping upstream cannot always be guaranteed.

Antlers at dawn

The rut of the red and fallow deer is one of the great British autumnal spectacles, providing a combination of sight and sound hard to rival in any season, let alone at this supposedly quieter time of year.

For both male and female deer, the rut is the most crucial part of their annual lifecycle. It provides an opportunity for both sexes to reproduce, and therefore pass on their genetic heritage down the generations. If they miss out – as the majority of males do – they may never get another chance to breed.

Two species, red and fallow deer, each take part in communal gatherings known as 'ruts'. The red deer rut generally begins in September, but peaks in October, though the timing does vary from year to year depending on weather conditions. Having shed their antlers in the spring, the males have now regrown a new set, with a span of as much as a metre. The number of 'points' on a set of antlers is crucial: the more points there are, the more dominant the stag; and in general the larger the antlers and the more points they have, the older the animal. During the spring and summer red deer live in smaller, separate herds containing either males or females, but as autumn arrives they begin to gather together in larger, mixed groups in preparation for the rut. The start of the rut is signalled by loud bellowing from the dominant stags, and then answered by the rival males. Given that the red deer is our largest terrestrial mammal, with the biggest stags weighing in at more than 220 kilograms, the scene is set for a spectacular contest.

For the next month or so, males will face up to one another several times a day, as they fight amongst themselves or – if they are feeling very brave – embarking on a bout with the dominant stag. This involves the challenger approaching the incumbent, and facing one another while uttering their loud, roaring calls. The size and volume of the dominant stag may be enough to see the challenger off; but if he thinks he may have a chance, then battle commences with the locking of horns. The bout can get

The annual red deer rut is one of the greatest spectacles of the autumn calendar, as males square up to one another in a bid to become the dominant stag and win the lion's share of the females.

quite violent, especially if the two stags are evenly matched; but eventually one of the combatants – usually the incumbent stag – will triumph and the other will turn tail and run away.

Females and non-breeding younger males stand around on the sidelines watching the action; though the females play a vital role as they will decide which stag they mate with. The rutting can take place at any time of day, though it usually peaks around dawn and dusk. The largest ruts are at the red deer 'hotspots' of the Scottish Highlands, Exmoor, the New Forest, and the semi-feral herds in deer parks at Fountains Abbey in Yorkshire, Woburn in Buckinghamshire and Richmond Park in London.

The rut of the red and fallow deer is one of the great British autumnal spectacles, providing a combination of sight and sound hard to rival in any season.

This is a 'winner takes all' situation: generally the dominant stag will get to mate with all available females in his harem, who have chosen him because he has proved himself in the rut. Thus they ensure they have provided the best possible genetic material for their calf, which will be born the following spring.

Occasionally the dominant stag will be past his prime, providing an opportunity for a younger male to take his place. In these situations the rutting is even more prolonged and intense, as rival males fight for the right to displace the leader.

The smaller fallow deer also take part in an annual rut each autumn, which usually reaches its peak a week or two later than that of their larger cousin. Male fallow deer have broad, palmate (hand-shaped) antlers, and often spend a lot of the time marking their territory by scraping their antlers across the ground. Being a smaller and lighter animal their contests are not usually quite so fierce or spectacular as the clash of the red deer males.

Again, the females may appear to be passive bystanders, but in fact they will make the choice of mate depending on the performance of the males. Once the rut is over, the victorious male mates with the females, each of which gives birth to a single fawn the following summer.

Fallow deer are a familiar sight in the British countryside, yet are not a native species, but were brought here by the Normans for hunting.

Fleeting fungi

On a damp autumn morning, as the mists begin to clear, what looks like a miracle occurs. Organisms sprout from the earth overnight, instantly festooning our fields and woodlands. They come in a wide range of sizes, shapes and colours: from tiny, pale individuals barely a couple of centimetres high to huge, colourful ones the size and shape of dinner plates.

The appearance of fungi – known commonly as mushrooms and toadstools – may appear miraculous, but it is just one small aspect of these organisms' complex and intricate lifecycle. For most of the year they remain underground, only emerging briefly above the earth from September to November.

It was long assumed that fungi were simply an unusual branch of the plant kingdom, but we now know that they are entirely separate, despite their superficial resemblance to plants. Whereas the vast majority of plants obtain their energy through the process of photosynthesis, fungi cannot do so, and instead find it in decaying matter in the soil. They stretch underground for huge distances, and the clusters of fungi we see on the surface are only the visible aspect of their existence, and a tiny fraction of the entire organism.

From the earliest times, primitive human beings have picked mushrooms for food, but one downside was that their location is highly unpredictable, both from year to year and place to place, though some spots are more favoured than others. Another – and much greater – problem is that many fungi are inedible or, worse still, highly poisonous.

The names of fungi reflect both our fear of and fascination with these extraordinary organisms. From the gruesome death cap to the intriguing blushing bracket, and the chanterelle to the wood blewit, the names have a poetic quality. Many, such as cep, chanterelle and morel, derive from French – reflecting the far greater popularity of edible fungi on the continent.

Some, such as the orange peel and hoof fungi, or the parasol mushroom, were named after their resemblance to another familiar object. Others, including the honey fungus, sulphur tuft and tawny grisette, got their name from their colour, while there are no prizes for guessing why the stinkhorn was so named.

Mushrooms and toadstools do not linger, as their role is simply to enable the underground fungi to reproduce. They do so either by producing spores, which are blown by the wind, or by being eaten and later excreted by a bird or mammal, both of which enable the fungus to spread to new areas. Heavy rainfall or frosts will soon damage the fruiting bodies, and once they finally disappear they will remain out of sight until the following autumn.

A striking cluster of sulphur tuft fungi growing on a mossy log – these are the fruiting bodies of much larger organisms below ground.

Trees through the seasons

No vista is complete without a tree; it provides the perfect punctuation mark in an otherwise level landscape. Throughout the year an evergreen provides an unvarying focal point, but deciduous trees delight us with their changing display. From green to russets to bare branches and back to green again, we can see the seasons shift through their appearance.

The last harvest

Autumn sees the peak of fruit production in commercial orchards, wild hedgerows and in our own gardens and allotments. Even when the bulk of this produce has been harvested, there is always windfall fruit to be found lying unpicked on the ground beneath the trees.

This discarded fruit provides an autumnal bounty for many creatures. Blackbirds and thrushes – which prefer feeding on the ground rather than on bird tables or hanging feeders – peck at rotting apples, pears and plums; while small mammals such as bank voles and wood mice also take their fill.

On warm days in September and October, insects gather to feed on the fermenting juices produced by these decaying fruits. Wasps and their larger relatives, hornets, are joined by a range of butterflies, including one of our largest and most impressive species: the red admiral.

Unlike most of our summer butterflies, the red admiral is a migrant, so some individuals will soon be heading south to their ancestral home around the shores of the Mediterranean. So the chance to stock up on the sugar-rich juices of fallen fruit is a real bonus. The only drawback is that when fruit ferments some of the sugar turns into alcohol; which is why on sunny autumn days some red admirals have a distinctly wonky flight!

Early autumn is also the peak season for berries – the fleshy fruit of shrubs and bushes – including elderberries, hawthorn berries, sloes and blackberries. But some plants delay producing their fruit until much later in the year, when there are plenty of hungry birds around who are able to distribute the seeds within, and as a result these plants have become closely associated with the festive season. The best known of these are holly, with its sharp, glossy-green leaves and bright red, shiny berries; ivy, whose berries are small and black; and mistletoe, with its clusters of white berries. All these have given rise to folklore, rhymes and beliefs which link the appearance of the fruit with this special time of year.

The holly and the ivy are traditionally linked together in the well-known Christmas carol, the origins of which go back many centuries. King Henry VIII, an accomplished amateur musician, also linked the two plants in another traditional song, one that laments the passing of the green foliage in the wood and welcomes the appearance of these two evergreen plants as the year comes to a quiet close.

During the Christmas season, sprigs of both holly and ivy were traditionally brought into homes to ward off evil, a superstition that is thought to date from before Christianity. The holly's combination of sharp, thorny leaves also led to

Bramblings are the northern cousins of the chaffinch, visiting Britain in winter from their breeding grounds in Scandinavia, sometimes in large flocks.

it being associated with Christ's Crown of Thorns, and its bright red berries with drops of his blood.

Ivy, a common climbing plant often found on the walls of homes and churches, has an equally long tradition linking it with the festive season. The berries, like those of holly, are also a very important source of food for wintering songbirds, especially thrushes, while earlier on in the autumn the flowers attract wasps and other insects on warm sunny days.

Likewise, mistletoe plays a crucial role both in our history and our natural history. Unlike holly and ivy, mistletoe is a parasitic plant, growing high in the branches of a tree: often apple, but also found on oak, lime and poplar trees. Because it is an evergreen, it is much more noticeable in late autumn and winter once the host tree's leaves have been shed. This is also the time of year that the mistletoe produces its fruit: clumps of white, sticky berries.

So it is hardly surprising that the mistletoe is, like the holly and ivy, closely linked with the festive season: specifically in the custom of hanging a sprig of mistletoe above a doorframe, or holding it over a person's head, and then requesting a kiss as a forfeit. Mistletoe was also thought to bring fertility, so women would wear a sprig around their necks or wrists in order to help them conceive. And like holly and ivy, it was regarded as a safeguard against evil, especially by the ancient druids, many of whose beliefs were taken up by Christians and survive as superstitions to this day.

Like holly and ivy, mistletoe was regarded as a safeguard against evil, especially by the ancient druids, many of whose beliefs survive as superstitions to this day.

Mistletoe has long been linked with birds: notably the aptly named mistle thrush. At 27 centimetres long, this is the largest British member of the thrush family, and is noticeably larger, paler and greyer than its cousin the song thrush. It was once believed that mistletoe seeds would only germinate if they had first passed through the guts of a bird such as a mistle thrush. We now know this not to be true: indeed, mistletoe readily grows on the branches of any of its host trees without the need for a bird to act as intermediary. Nevertheless, mistle thrushes (and other birds) do help the mistletoe by eating the berries and then spreading the seeds to other locations.

The bank vole is one of our commonest mammals, but like other small rodents it is rarely seen. This animal is enjoying a harvest of sweet chestnuts.

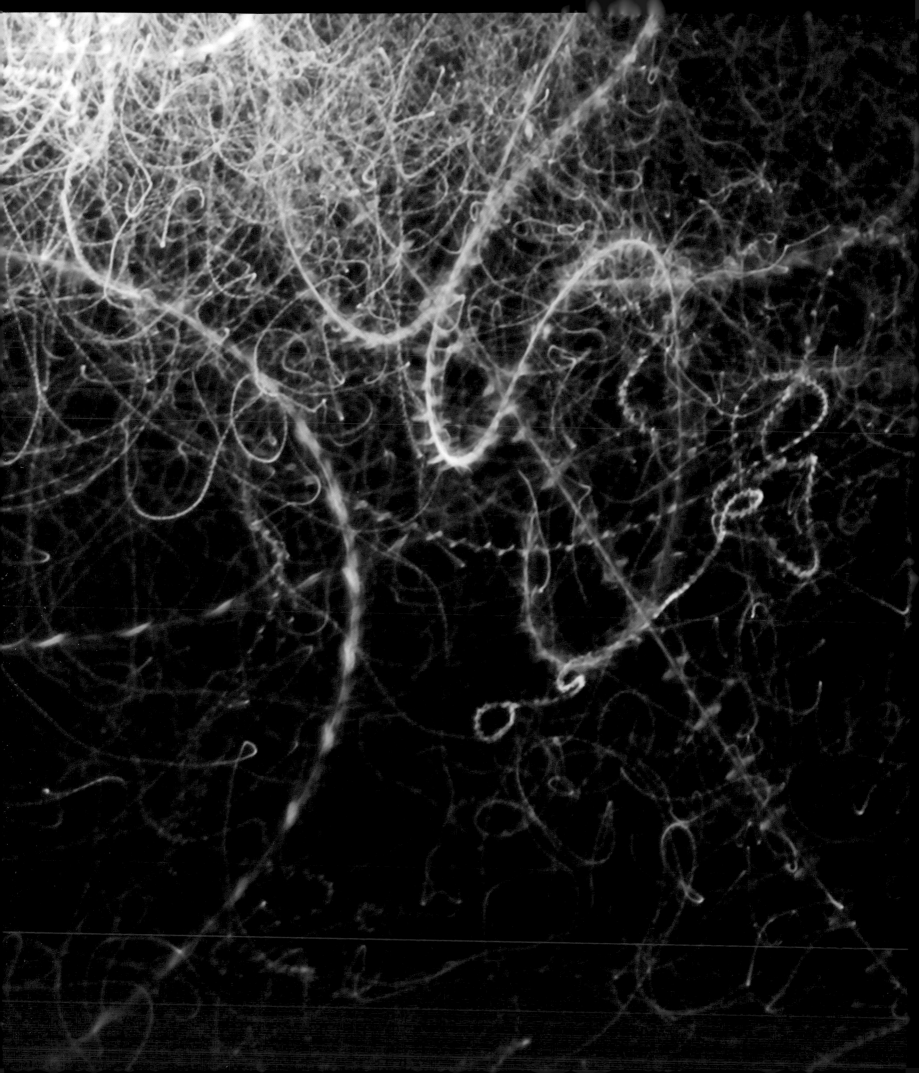

Winter moths

Moths are generally associated with warm, muggy summer nights rather than the cooler seasons of autumn and winter. So it comes as something of a surprise to see these winged insects fluttering in the car headlights, or caught in the beam of a security light during the colder months, when we are not used to seeing any insects on the wing.

Yet several species of moth do not usually emerge as adults until October, November or even December. Their names reflect their late appearance: they include the November moth, autumnal moth and the winter moth.

Even by moth standards these species are particularly drab to look at: mainly greyish-brown in shade, though a closer look reveals subtle and delicate markings which create a very pleasing pattern. The males have rounded wings, and are between 20 and 30 millimetres across, whereas the females have tiny wings and are unable to fly.

Autumn and winter moths may sometimes be seen in the hour or so just before dusk, but they mostly emerge after dark. Like all nocturnal moths they are attracted to bright lights, and may appear in large numbers, especially on cloudy, moonless nights when an artificial source of light will be brighter t han any natural one. They are able to fly at extremely low temperatures, even managing to get airborne when the thermometer falls close to freezing point.

They can do this because they have unusually large and well-developed flight muscles, which they use to vibrate their wings rapidly before take-off, so they can raise their body temperature to a level required to get and remain airborne. Their body is also covered with dense scales, which enables them to retain heat more easily.

Once the male has found a female and mated, she will lay her eggs on a crevice in the bark of a twig, often near a leaf bud. Both male and female die soon afterwards, and the eggs do not hatch for another few months, when spring temperatures have reached 13°C or so.

The movement of moths at night is caught in the beam of a car light, their trails visible against the dark night sky.

Safety in numbers

The starling is not usually a contender for Britain's favourite bird. Often denounced as a 'bird-table bully', its gawky appearance and tuneless whistling does not make it endearing. However, while from a distance starlings appear rather drab, their plumage is actually a striking combination of dark glossy feathers and tiny pale spots.

Although starlings are one of our commonest breeding birds, they have been in serious decline in recent years, as industrial farming practices have killed off the insects and grubs in the soil on which starlings feed. But in autumn and winter the British population is joined by millions of starlings from farther north and east – mainly from Arctic Russia, where conditions are too cold for the birds to find food and survive during the bitter Siberian winter.

During the day, they feed in a wide range of habitats, including grassy fields, muddy estuaries and of course our gardens. But as dusk falls, they leave these areas and join together in flocks, heading purposefully towards their roost sites. These may be in towns and cities, where the warmth of buildings increases the birds' chances of survival; or in areas of woodland, where they can spend the night in the twigs and branches of bare trees. But the biggest – and most famous – roost of all is amongst the reedbeds on the Somerset Levels; former peat diggings transformed by conservationists into a series of vast nature reserves.

The starlings begin to arrive an hour or so before dusk: small flocks at first, followed by larger and larger ones, sometimes numbering in the tens of thousands. But instead of going immediately to roost, the birds often perform incredible aerial displays, delighting hundreds of observers with their acrobatic performances. For a brief period, as the winter sun begins to drop beneath the horizon, they twist and turn like shoals of fish, creating extraordinary amoeba-like patterns against the darkening sky. They remain silent during these displays, apart from the collective rush of air passing beneath millions of wings; a sound which has given rise to the collective name for a flock of starlings: known as a 'murmuration'.

Of course these displays are not for our benefit: they are a sign of each individual starling weighing up its best chance of survival in case of the arrival of a predator such as a falcon or hawk. By staying close to its neighbours, each bird maximises its chances of avoiding attack. At the same time, it – along with its millions of companions – is assessing the best place to roost for the night.

Hence the flock behaves rather like a single, giant bird rather than a collection of individuals. Finally, when it is almost too dark to see the ground below, the flock descends into the reeds; a few at first, followed by a great onrush. Then the noise begins to build: a crescendo of chattering, before they finally fall asleep.

OPPOSITE: In autumn and winter starlings gather in noisy, sociable feeding flocks, often dominating garden bird tables and feeding stations.

FOLLOWING PAGES: Starlings wait for darkness to descend before they leave their perches to find somewhere to sleep for the night.

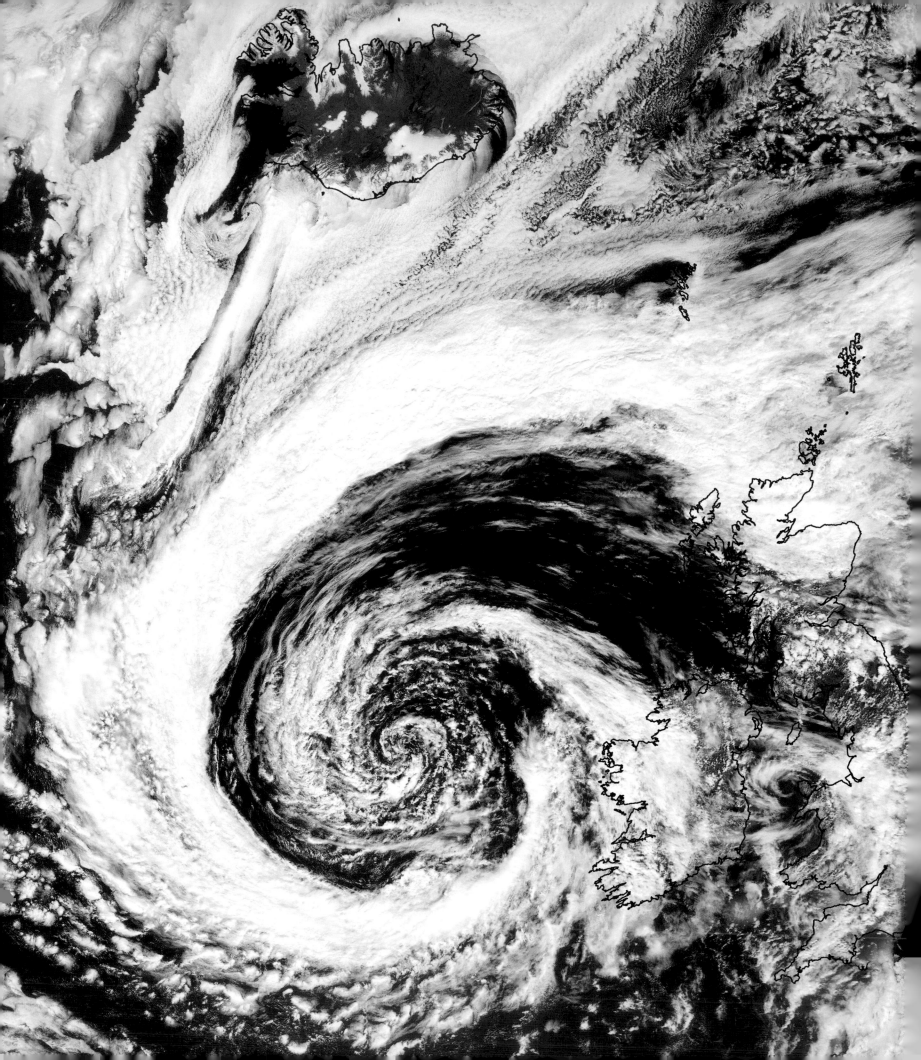

Autumn storms can be quite dramatic in their power and destruction. This seafront at Lyme Regis, Dorset, faces the mighty waves head on (below).

Chattering companions

Another bird that roosts in large numbers in winter is the pied wagtail. This behaviour is perhaps more surprising in this species because it is generally known as one of nature's loners.

This small, neat songbird with its perpetually moving tail and black-and-white plumage is usually seen on its own, walking methodically across a close-cut lawn or town pavement in search of food. Occasionally, when another wagtail gets too close, these birds fly up into the air in a minor skirmish, before going off in their separate directions. But as the autumn nights draw in, the pied wagtail changes its behaviour dramatically and becomes a very social animal. As dusk begins to fall, the darkening sky is dotted with little shapes like musical notes on a stave; all heading in the same direction, and uttering their penetrating, two-note call as they fly.

By late November and December, in city centres up and down the country, shoppers frantically hunt for Christmas gifts, staggering home beneath the weight of their purchases. Yet in their rush, few have the time or energy to look upwards to see this seasonal phenomenon: the gathering of pied wagtails in their roost.

The birds usually head towards the same, regular site every year: often an ornamental tree with dense foliage, planted by town planners to bring a little greenery and colour into the grey urban environment. Elsewhere, pied wagtails also gather at motorway service stations or on industrial estates.

These seemingly unwelcoming sites have two main things in common: light and heat. Light acts as a deterrent to predators such as owls, which otherwise might be tempted by the prospect of grabbing an easy meal. Heat – from the roofs of buildings or simply the sheer mass of people coming and going beneath the roost site – also helps these tiny birds to survive the cold nights, as they huddle together for added warmth.

While the huge starling roosts or the gatherings of wintering ducks, geese and swans may be better known to many, there is a certain quiet charm about the less showy pied wagtail roost. As night falls, the chattering sound of the birds begins to subside, and by the time the shops have closed and people have made their way home, all is quiet. But there may now be more than a thousand wagtails gathered together in this one place, as oblivious to the departing hordes of people below as the humans are to the birds above them.

Pied wagtails gather in large flocks on autumn and winter evenings in order to roost together for safety and warmth.

The Highland tiger

Of all Britain's wild creatures, few are as mysterious, elusive and scarce as the Scottish wildcat. Other top mammal predators such as the wolf, bear and lynx have long been extinct in Britain, but the wildcat has managed to cling on in the remote highlands of Scotland. However, now it too has become a threatened species.

Wildcats were once found throughout the wilds of England and Wales, as well as in Scotland, but as the human population of these islands grew, so the wildcats fell victim to loss of their forest habitat and persecution: both because of the threat they posed to domestic lambs and gamebirds, and also because the animals' thick fur was widely prized.

They had vanished from southern Britain by the Tudor era (sixteenth century), and by the late nineteenth century the species had retreated further into the remote glens and forests of the highlands of Scotland, where it became known as the 'Highland tiger'.

Wildcats are larger than domestic cats, reaching up to one metre long (including the tail, which is about one-third of their total length). They can weigh up to 7.5 kilograms, and live for a decade or more. Although they look very similar to tabby-coloured domestic cats, they can be told apart by a combination of features, including their larger size and thickset build, and a thick, bushy tail with a series of concentric black bands along its length and a black tip.

Wildcats produce a single litter of up to seven kittens in the spring, which become mature the following winter. Until this time, despite having their mother's protection, they are very vulnerable to attack by predators such as golden eagles, stoats and foxes.

Once they reach maturity, wildcats are generally solitary animals and hunt by night, stalking small mammals such as mice and voles as well as larger prey such as rabbits and hares, which they despatch with their razor-sharp teeth. In late autumn and winter wildcats take advantage of snowfalls, which enable them to creep up on their quarry as the other creatures search desperately for food; and also thrive at this time of year on the growing availability of carrion, as birds and mammals die of starvation because of the icy conditions.

In recent years wildcats have benefitted from more enlightened attitudes of gamekeepers and landowners, leading to a drop in persecution. But another, even more serious threat has emerged: the presence of feral domestic cats. It is thought that there are around two million feral cats in Britain, of which about 100,000 live in the Scottish Highlands, alongside the Scottish wildcat.

OPPOSITE: The Scottish wildcat is one of the rarest of all our mammals, and thanks to crossbreeding with feral domestic cats they may now even be extinct in their pure form.

FOLLOWING PAGES: Fallow deer have learnt to make the most of what is on offer in winter, munching through a layer of frost to reach the grass beneath.

Unfortunately, when feral cats and wildcats meet they often interbreed, which means that the gene pool of these wild animals is rapidly becoming diluted. Conservationists believe that there are now fewer than 400 purebred Scottish wildcats in existence, and the true number may be even lower than this. Because the Scottish wildcat is a distinct subspecies from its counterparts in mainland Europe and Asia, it is irreplaceable. If this crucial predator does disappear, an important link will have been lost in the whole of the highland ecosystem.

Some conservationists are now proposing a radical plan to prevent the Scottish wildcat becoming extinct. This would entail trapping wildcats and testing their genes, and then taking the 'best' animals into captivity to crossbreed them, producing offspring that are as close to purebred wildcats as possible. At the same time any feral cats in the wildcats' habitat would be trapped, and either neutered or killed. This may seem a controversial solution, but it is likely to be the only way by which this magnificent animal can ultimately be saved.

Little robin redbreast

The robin is also closely associated with Christmas, often appearing on cards sent during the festive season. This appears to have arisen in an unusual way: early postmen wore red uniforms, and were nicknamed 'robins'. Victorian artists then put robins on the cards themselves; the bird usually depicted carrying an envelope in its bill. The association with Christmas soon stuck.

The robin is, without question, Britain's best-loved bird, regularly topping any opinion poll that is carried out to find the nation's favourite. This is in no small part down to its habit of coming into our gardens and boldly hopping around our doorsteps, especially when temperatures drop and food becomes hard to find.

Robins are known as 'the gardener's friend', but it might be more accurate to call the gardener 'the robin's friend', as the bird benefits from our hard work in turning over the soil, enabling it to sneak in and grab an earthworm or beetle revealed by the spade. It has long puzzled ornithologists that British robins are particularly prone to following humans, whereas continental European robins are much shyer and rarely approach people. The answer appears to lie in two factors: first, the British love of gardening, which provides countless opportunities for human–bird interactions; and second, the scarcity of other large mammals such as wild boars in Britain, which the robin would have followed around as they turned over the soil in woods and forests instead.

Oddly, though, some people do not want robins too close. If a robin comes into the home itself this is traditionally regarded as very bad luck, supposedly resulting in the death of one of the household's occupants. Yet strangely, other people hold a contradictory opinion and regard the appearance of a robin indoors as a positive omen, especially if it closely follows the death of a loved one.

Another contradiction in our nation's love of robins is that of all our garden birds they are amongst the feistiest, most aggressive and sometimes even downright violent. Male robins are very reluctant to allow a rival male robin into their territory, and will immediately attack any intruders, sometimes fighting to the death in order to preserve their dominance. Many people know this, and yet continue to see this dumpy, colourful and undoubtedly cute little bird as a friendly visitor to their back doorstep!

The final reason why robins are such a perennial favourite is also linked to their territorial behaviour. Unlike other songbirds, which generally flock together in the winter months, robins defend a territory throughout the year – and so need to sing during autumn and winter as well as spring and summer. For us, the sound of a robin's song at dusk on a chilly winter's afternoon is a reminder of the joys of the spring to come.

The robin is traditionally associated with Christmas, perhaps because this bird's confident habits mean that it often comes to our door steps in search of food, especially in harsh winter weather.

BEHIND
THE
SCENES

It takes skill and determination to be a wildlife filmmaker and bring the natural world to our screens. Behind the scenes there is an army of crew and dedicated professionals who battle our changing climate and often wild weather as well as the unpredictable nature of our birds, animals and insects to tell the story of their life through the seasons in *The Great British Year*.

MANY PROFESSIONAL FILMMAKERS are widely travelled: series such as *Planet Earth*, *Frozen Planet* and *Africa* are made in some of the most remote and inaccessible places on the planet. This work requires military-style logistics; weeks, months and sometimes years in the field; and a willingness on behalf of the producers and camera crews to endure physical hardship and discomfort in their quest to bring formerly unseen behaviour to our screens.

So you might be forgiven for assuming that the team behind *The Great British Year* had it easy. After all, their subject matter could not have been closer to home: our own native land, Britain, and its wildlife, seen through the four seasons of the year.

It is true that filming wildlife in Britain is usually easier than doing so abroad. There are no long-distance flights to arrange, no complex and arcane customs rules to fall foul of, and no dangerous war zones to pass through.

Another huge advantage of filming at home is that Britain is, without question, a nation obsessed with wildlife in all its forms. Britain's wildlife has been studied and surveyed, poked and prodded, watched and above all loved, for more than 200 years; ever since the Hampshire vicar Gilbert White wrote about the seasonal events in his home village in *The Natural History of Selborne*.

Since then we Brits have led the world in three areas: the scientific study of plants and animals, their conservation, and last but not least, the recreational hobby of watching wildlife. The RSPB has more than one million members, the Wildlife Trusts close to that number, and as a result there are legions of professional and amateur observers who together have contributed to making ours the best-known fauna and flora in the world.

For filmmakers doing a series about British wildlife, this has huge advantages. Production teams from the BBC Natural History Unit are able to call on an army of enthusiastic and knowledgeable experts, either through the BBC's partner organisations such as the National Trust, the British Trust for Ornithology, and the Wildfowl and Wetlands Trust, or through local naturalists who

have dedicated their lives to studying the great green bush-cricket, say, or the barn owl.

Over the years, this invaluable resource of experts has enabled the BBC to make many memorable British wildlife series, including *The Living Isles* (1986), *Living Britain* (1999), *British Isles: a Natural History* (2004) and *The Nature of Britain* (2007).

Without this army of naturalists up and down the country, series such as these would have been far less rich in content. These local experts can not only tell the production team everything they need to know about a particular species, but more importantly they can direct them to the best place at the optimum time in order to potentially capture the elusive creature on camera.

The BBC Natural History Unit – and indeed all wildlife filmmakers – owes a huge debt to these unsung heroes; without them a series such as *The Great British Year* could never be made, as we shall discover in this chapter.

So with all these advantages over their globetrotting colleagues, did *The Great British Year* team spend a

leisurely two years wandering the country with their cameras, as the wildlife queued up to be captured for posterity? Of course not. Making wildlife programmes is never easy, and although the team enjoyed the advantages of filming on home turf, they also suffered some very practical problems.

These fell broadly into three categories: time, money and the weather. The whole series was conceived, planned, shot and edited in less than two years, and on a very tight budget – the filming costs for a whole episode of *The Great British Year* were about the same as for a single sequence in *Africa*. But of all the problems the team had to overcome, by far the trickiest were those posed by the British weather. Because this series focuses on the changes between the four seasons of the year, the team had to plan even more carefully than usual. They knew that if they missed a particular event or behaviour the first time, they might never get another chance to film it again.

Britain's weather and our seasons are famously unpredictable. In some parts of the country, such as

the Cairngorm Mountains in Scotland, it is not unknown to experience 'four seasons in one day', with sunshine, rain, gale-force winds and snow all making an appearance during a 24-hour period. Added to this the recent topsy-turvy seasons and extreme weather, almost certainly caused by global climate change, and it becomes clear that nothing can be taken for granted. Unlike actors, wildlife doesn't work to a script – even when you are in the right place at the right time, nature doesn't always play ball!

So the team had to be able to respond immediately: for example when snow was forecast they had to mobilise their camera people instantly. If they waited even 24 hours the snow might have melted and their opportunity would be gone, perhaps forever.

With a production team based in Bristol, in the southwest corner of the country, this was not always practicable. Britain may be relatively small compared with, say, Africa, but it still takes a long time to get from Bristol to Shetland or South Uist; or even, given our crowded roads, to Kent or Essex! Knowing *what* might happen with a particular species is easy to discover; knowing *where* and especially *when* is much more tricky!

James Brickell, series producer of *The Great British Year*, is an old hand at wildlife filmmaking. His credits include the BAFTA-winning David Attenborough series on reptiles and amphibians, *Life in Cold Blood*; the hugely successful CBBC series *Deadly 60*, presented by Steve Backshall; and most recently a three-part series on *The Great Barrier Reef*, during which James and his young family decamped to Australia for more than a year.

Brickell has filmed all over the world: from the freezing Arctic wastes of Alaska to the baking deserts of Arizona, and from steaming jungles in Borneo to deep beneath many of the world's oceans. Along the way, he has encountered venomous snakes, ghost bats, polar bears and tiger sharks. Yet he believes that *The Great British Year* has been the greatest challenge of his career:

'With projects I've worked on before, the chances of success were increased by controlling as many factors as I could, through good planning and research. But trying to capture the best and worst of the British weather using a traditional approach is a bit like trying to win the world's toughest game of cards – even if you and your team do a great job it still comes down to chance.'

Yet James and his colleagues love a challenge, and between them they worked long and hard to ensure that they could overcome the many barriers they faced and bring us the wonderful series we can now enjoy.

This is the story of how they did so, told largely through the experiences, and in the words, of those involved.

It is a story full of surprises. For as well as employing cutting-edge technology and using it in new and different ways, and along with taking advantages of the existing network of amateur naturalists up and down the country, the team also adopted the latest developments in social media. This enabled them to mobilise a crack team of amateur filmmakers all over the country, who could be there on the ground at exactly the right time to capture something truly special.

But first, they had to overcome the greatest challenge of all, and something close to all our hearts: the good old British weather!

Weird weather

Britain's weather is notoriously fickle and unpredictable: we can have snow in June and an Indian summer in November; freezing winters that go on until April, and mild wet ones that end in February; storms, gales, droughts and floods – sometimes, as in 2012, all of these during the course of a single year.

Our weather is so varied and unpredictable for one simple reason: the British Isles is situated on the western edge of the vast landmass of Eurasia, in mid-latitudes, with a huge ocean, the Atlantic, to our west.

Depending on the prevailing winds and weather systems, we can experience low pressure with wind and rain from the west; warm, Saharan breezes from the south; brisk dry winds from the east; or freezing Arctic weather from the north – often within a single season and sometimes during a single week!

During the period leading up to autumn 2011, when *The Great British Year* series first went into production, through to late summer 2013, when the final frame was shot, Britain experienced the most bizarre period of weather since records began. The winter of 2009–10 was the coldest of the twenty-first century so far, and the fifth or sixth coldest in 100 years, with heavy and prolonged snowfalls across much of the country. Then came spring 2011, which was the warmest and earliest on record and rolled through summer into an autumn and winter which became one of the longest periods of drought in southern and eastern Britain since records began. Yorkshire, for example, experienced the driest 12 months on record, while more than 20 million people were subject to hosepipe bans. Then almost as soon as drought was officially declared in April 2012, the weather turned – dramatically. Despite the dry first three months of 2012, the year was the wettest on record in England, and by a whisker the second wettest on record in the UK as a whole. The year closed with a winter that was mostly mild and wet, with very little snow.

All this unpredictable and unexpected weather had major – and largely negative – consequences for *The Great British Year* filming schedule. For example, after two snowy winters before the production began, the two years when they were filming were largely snow-free, apart from in the highlands of Scotland.

Spring and summer were even worse: constant rain during 2012 made it almost impossible to schedule shoots of specific seasonal behaviours. Many shoots had to be cancelled at the last minute, or even called off on the day,

A wildlife cameraman braves the wintry weather in his quest for picture-perfect footage of red deer in the snow.

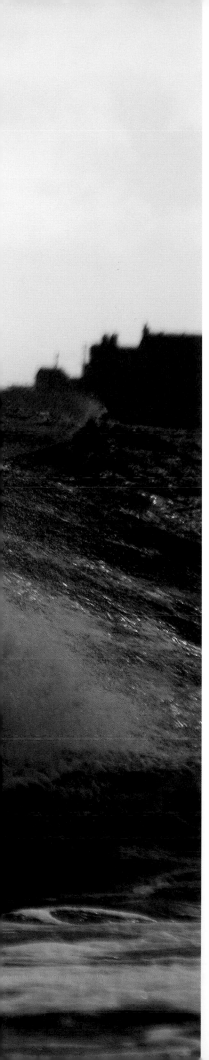

because of the bad weather, adding unnecessary expense to the production, and extra stress for the team, as assistant producer Jo Avery explains:

'At first we were playing catch-up, as key spring events were happening several weeks earlier than usual, so we were in danger of missing them.'

Then, almost as soon as the government issued drought orders on 5 April, came the twist that no one could have foreseen: the heavens opened and soon the droughts turned to floods, causing devastation across large swathes of the countryside. For Jo and the team, this was equally calamitous:

'Animals were dying, the countryside was in chaos, and the whole country seemed to be under water – it really did feel like Mission Impossible!'

One example sums up the frustrations and difficulties faced by the team. For the Spring into Summer episode they wanted to follow the progress of one of Britain's largest and most spectacular seabird colonies, on the Farne Islands off the coast of Northumberland. The first seabirds arrive back from their wintering sites out in the open ocean in late March, and must raise their young in the brief window of opportunity that follows. So wildlife cameraman Lindsay McCrae planned to spend time living on the islands, getting to know the birds as individuals, and following their struggle in this race to reproduce:

'I've been filming wildlife all my life, watching the seasons and how the landscape and wild creatures adapt to the changes that happen day by day. The British weather changes all the time, so I'm used to having to react quickly, but I've never known a year like 2012.'

Lindsay first attempted to get onto the islands in mid-March, aiming to film the empty cliff faces before the hordes of birds returned. But with the unseasonably warm March weather came fog, and all boats to the Farnes were cancelled.

After hitching a lift on a dive boat, Lindsay finally reached the islands: only to discover that the birds had already been present for a fortnight, and had firmly established their territories on the cliffs. Even though he had arrived in what he had thought would be plenty of time, the early spring had scuppered his plans.

Two months later, in mid-May, Lindsay made his second trip to the Farnes. By now, there had been more than a month of rain and wind, and once again bad weather made just getting to the islands a challenge. Lindsay did manage to get

Wild weather and stormy waves along our coastline can play havoc with the seasonal routines of wildlife – as well as with a filming schedule!

across, but unfortunately the rest of the crew – and his precious camera kit – were left behind on the mainland.

Once again, on arrival he discovered that the weather was causing havoc with the team's plans – having been two weeks early in March, the birds were now running two weeks late in their seasonal activities! There was nothing to be done but wait and hope that the weather cleared, as Lindsay recalls:

'At this point the birds should have been feeding young, with lots of activity to film at the nest – instead the eggs hadn't even hatched yet and the birds were just sitting tight.'

The puffins' burrows had been flooded out, and kittiwakes and shags had also suffered the effects of the constant storms. Worst hit was one of the key species on the Farnes, the Arctic tern. They had only just arrived to begin their courtship displays, when they should have been sitting on eggs or feeding chicks. This could have proved fatal for these global travellers, as once the chicks have hatched it is a race against time for them to grow quickly enough to undertake the longest migratory journey of any of the world's birds, all the way to Antarctica. So when Lindsay was eventually reunited with his camera, he had nothing to film, and he was then stuck on the islands once more to sit out yet another storm.

Meanwhile, back on the mainland the team were in a race against time to film all the bustling activity of a British spring, rushing to every corner of the UK to capture the season's progress.

One challenge was to use a thermal imaging camera, which enables us to see the heat given off by a wild animal at night. The plan was to film one of our rarest bats, the greater horseshoe, in the Wye Valley in southeast Wales as they left the caves where they had hibernated over winter.

Unfortunately, once again the timing was thrown into confusion by the weird weather. The warm March meant that the bats had left the roost far earlier than usual, so instead of capturing a spectacle of hundreds of bats, the thermal camera only registered six individuals. To add insult to injury, the rain then began to fall, and almost as soon as these half-dozen bats had departed, they had second thoughts and flew back into the cave!

By June, the floods were worse than ever. James was trying to film blue sharks off the coast of Cornwall, where he needed fine, calm weather and flat seas just to have a chance of seeing these elusive fish, let alone filming them.

Meanwhile, elsewhere producer Bridget Appleby was attempting to film one of our greatest spring spectacles: the emergence of mayflies on a warm, sunny day.

Not only was it hardly ever warm and sunny that summer, but Bridget was also trying to use an ultra-high-speed camera which captures action at an

The team were in a race against time to film all the bustling activity of a British spring, rushing to every corner of the UK to capture the season's progress.

Throughout 2012, droughts gave way to floods, leaving farmland and countryside under water across much of the country.

incredible 1,000 frames a second – enabling us to see the mayflies emerge forty times slower than the human eye can normally do.

But as Bridget points out, things didn't exactly go to plan:

'Mayflies are tiny insects, about the size of your thumbnail, and they move very fast. To capture them we needed a bright, sunny afternoon, with the sun behind the action so that cameramen Ed Edwards and Mark Payne-Gill could pick them out as they began to emerge from the water's surface. What we got was day after day of rain and wind – no good at all!'

Just as the combination of frustration and exhaustion was reaching its zenith, there was a brief moment of hope. The rain stopped, the sun came out – but would the mayflies still be emerging? Fortunately, they were. The crew was rapidly mobilised, the sun continued to shine, and the sequence was in the can at last!

With the summer solstice almost upon us, the team making the Spring into Summer episode had one last location to visit, or revisit – the Farne Islands. Tension was high: would any of the seabirds have survived this cruel and unrelenting weather? And if they had, would any of them have managed to raise their young?

Amazingly, the change in the weather had come just in time. The cliffs were full of guillemots and kittiwakes; puffins waddled comically around the feet of the production team, and the sun shone. Lindsay was finally able to capture a memorable sequence of these extraordinary birds.

Looking back, Lindsay learned some valuable lessons from the weirdest spring on record:

'I have such newfound respect for the wildlife of the UK. We have struggled every step of the way with the rain in 2012, and we don't have to live every day of our lives out in it, find food, and keep youngsters safe and warm. And next year all these seabirds will be back to start the race for life once again. Meanwhile, I'm going to sleep for the rest of the summer!'

The fickle weather of spring 2012 taught *The Great British Year* team a vital lesson: that to combat the problems it presented, and to get the production back on track to achieve their aims, they would need to develop new ways of working.

They did so by taking advantage of a new technology not available to their predecessors: not high-speed cameras or thermal imaging devices, but the social media – in particular, Twitter.

Skipper Colin Barnes and assistant producer Jo Avery (bottom left) navigate the *Holly Jo* while on the roof local whale expert Pádraig Whooley (left) and cameraman Matteo Willis (right) look out for fin whales.

Tweeting the twitchers

Email, Google, Wikipedia, Facebook and Twitter are so much part of our daily lives it is sometimes hard to remember what life was like without them. They make research far easier than before: the days when TV researchers relied on the telephone and 'snail mail' to communicate with the outside world are long gone, and feel like some curious chapter from our ancient past.

Yet it is worth remembering that we only started using email regularly in the late 1990s; that Google was not widely used until about a decade ago; and that Wikipedia (founded in 2001), Facebook (2004) and Twitter (2006) are barely out of their infancy! Given that all these new technologies were around for some years before they were generally adopted, it is fair to say that the last decade has seen a sea change in the way TV production teams go about researching and making their programmes.

The Great British Year series was fortunate to have a number of young, enthusiastic and technologically literate people in their team; and also that James Brickell and the (slightly) older members of the team were open to new ways of doing things. At first, James thought that Twitter might be a useful additional tool for the team; but he soon realised that it was central to them achieving their goals:

> 'Up to that time, my experience of social media had been very superficial. But it soon became obvious that we could use it to communicate with a network of people with incredibly valuable information and skills: hundreds of naturalists scattered all across Britain.'

At a stroke, the team had a way of finding and contacting people who were out in the countryside watching or photographing wildlife every single day, and having an ongoing conversation with them. As James puts it:

> 'Twitter enabled us to have eyes and ears all over Britain.'

In a world where we have become used to instant communication by mobile phone or email, Twitter takes this to a whole new level. With smartphones now routinely carried by most naturalists, Twitter's millions of followers can both report their sightings as they happen, and respond to requests from the TV production team.

This was put into practice using another massive improvement in technology. Digital photography has come on leaps and bounds since it first began to film a

BEHIND
THE
SCENES

284

With observers linked to technology across the country, the production team could be there with the action from dawn to dusk and into the night.

decade or so ago; and nowadays digital SLR (single-lens reflex) cameras costing a fraction of the price of professional video cameras are able to produce moving images of an extraordinarily high quality.

They can also be used to create stunning time-lapse images: in which a single frame is automatically exposed every few seconds or minutes. This allows the photographer to create a moving image showing the passage of time: clouds passing across the sky, or a scene changing from day to night, for example.

Here, Twitter helped once again: *The Great British Year* team could use the social networking site to assess the information they were getting on events in the field, and make requests to photographers to capture rapidly changing weather events such as snowfalls. And all from the comfort of their centrally heated office in Bristol.

The results add a crucial dimension to the series: given that seasons are all about the passage of time, they help to create a visual style that enables the viewer to experience the seasons rather than simply being told about them.

For the first episode, Winter into Spring, the team were looking for a story that illustrated the connection between seasons, wildlife and people, specifically during the winter, a time when many animals turn to us for feeding opportunities. Luke Massey, a young photographer, had been watching one of our most beautiful and spectacular birds of prey, red kites, on farmland in Oxfordshire. He watched the kites as they followed tractors exposing fresh earth as they ploughed, swooping down – sometimes almost between the blades of the plough – to grab juicy worms from the surface.

Since kites were reintroduced to the Chilterns two decades ago, this behaviour has become increasingly frequent, but nevertheless it is tricky to predict exactly when and where it will take place. Luke used Twitter to alert the team as soon as the kites began to gather, and wildlife cameraman Mark Yates was able to get to the scene within hours, to capture the dramatic sequence of more than 20 red kites dive-bombing a tractor over a misty field.

Some scenarios are hard to film simply because they occur so infrequently here in Britain. One such is the legendary Aurora Borealis – the Northern Lights – an amazing natural nighttime display of colourful flashes in the sky caused by the collision of charged particles with atoms in the atmosphere. Here the team enlisted the help of talented time-lapse photographer Barry Stewart. Based in Wick in the far north of Scotland, Barry was able to capture stunning images of this amazing phenomenon right on his doorstep, in the wilds of Caithness.

PREVIOUS PAGES: The team documented Britain's changing seasons from the air using a cineflex gyro-stabilised camera.

OPPOSITE: New camera technology means photographers can capture images of animals moving at a rapid rate, such as this osprey hunting for dinner in the Cairngorms National Park.

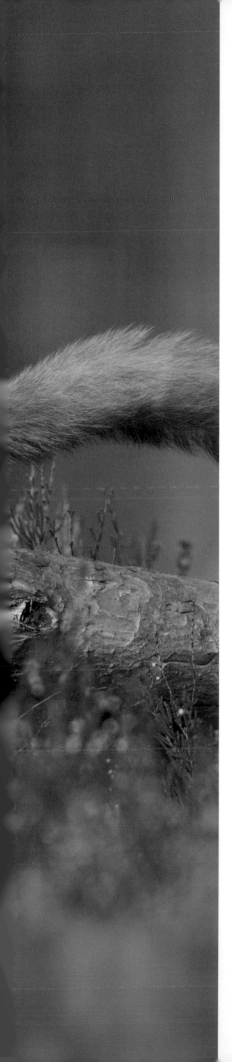

Another contributor, Tom Walker, was already an accomplished young landscape photographer with a passion for nature and a burning ambition to become a wildlife cameraman. But until *The Great British Year* team got in touch with him, he had never tried time-lapse photography before. So he decided to have a go at obtaining time-lapse sequences of various meteorological spectacles using his existing digital camera gear. Just six weeks after trying the technique for the very first time, he began submitting his work to the production office in Bristol. They immediately realised his potential for obtaining really striking sequences and enlisted him to work on more traditional shoots as well – thus helping him gain experience while creating some memorable material for the series.

Tom also had to learn to react quickly during these shoots: during one sudden storm he had to throw his jacket over his precious camera to stop it getting wet, thus ensuring a soaking for himself!

Without these immensely talented and dedicated people ... the visual style of *The Great British Year* series would have been far less rich and memorable.

Finally, Chad Gordon Higgins is an experienced time-lapse photographer, but rather than specialising in wildlife and natural history his chosen genre is stunning landscape shots for commercials and music videos.

However, Chad's creative skills were soon transferred to the very different world of nature photography, and his legendary patience born of hours spend waiting for a scene to be ready to shoot meant that he was perfect for some of the series' most complex and challenging time-lapses. These include tracking the sun's path across the famous London skyline, and the most ambitious sequence of the whole series: following an ancient Dorset oak through the course of a year, using a special rig that enabled him to move around the tree as time passed.

Without these immensely talented and dedicated people, there can be no doubt that the visual style of *The Great British Year* series would have been far less rich and memorable.

OPPOSITE: You never know when you will get the shot you want, but cameras can be set up and worked remotely to prevent human presence scaring off any passing animals.

FOLLOWING PAGES: Seals are naturally inquisitive creatures and are drawn to a diver and camera. With 40 per cent of the world's population of grey seals living in our seas, there was little doubt the team would find some to film.

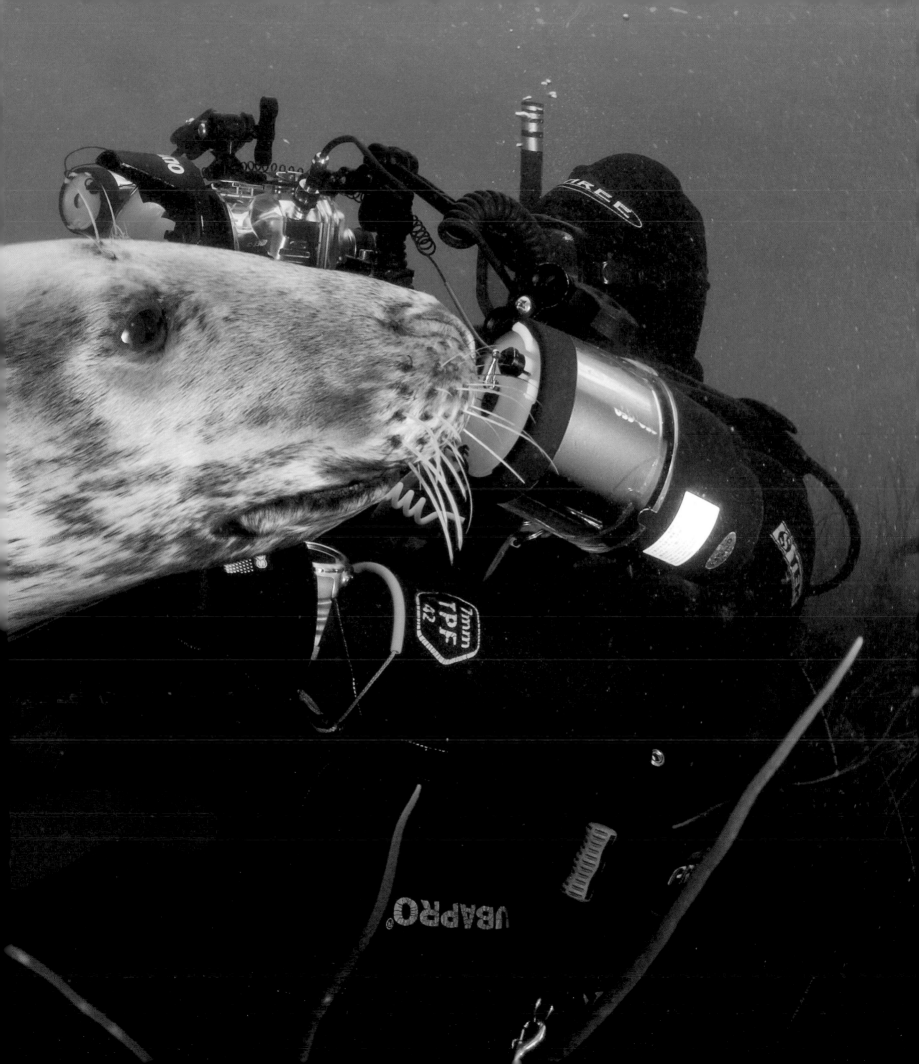

Chaos in the wake of climate change

Dealing with the fickle British weather is one thing; but how did *The Great British Year* team cope with one of the most controversial, unpredictable and frightening issues facing both us and the wildlife: global climate change? This impacts on wildlife filmmakers both logistically and editorially, and getting the balance right was always going to be a difficult task, as producer Elizabeth White points out:

> 'It's easy to get confused by the variations in the British weather – for example when we get a cold, snowy winter people begin to question the existence of global warming. But there's a big distinction between our weather, which can vary dramatically from year to year, and the long-term trends that make up our climate. This was something we were keen to cover in the series.'

Weather, climate and natural events are intimately linked: we mark the changing seasons with the first flowers in spring, the departing swallows in autumn, and the arrival of migrating ducks and geese in early winter. But now, as *The Great British Year* team discovered to their cost, we cannot rely on past timings of events to predict when they will occur. Fortunately, as Elizabeth reveals:

> 'As a nation, we're very much "tuned in" to seasonal events, and this information is proving really useful as we try to understand the changes that are happening here in Britain.'

Here are just a few examples of changes in the seasonal patterns of nature discovered by phenologists – professional scientists and their army of amateur observers who log seasonal events from year to year, and then analyse the data to reveal changes:

Oak budburst – appearing three weeks earlier than 60 years ago
Snowdrops – now flowering a whole month earlier than 50 years ago
Swallows – now arriving back from Africa nearly nine days earlier
    than 30 years ago
Blackbirds – nesting seven days earlier than 30 years ago
Ladybirds – emerging about two weeks earlier than 30 years ago

These observations demonstrate how nature is responding to the fact that spring is, on average, arriving earlier and earlier each decade. And this is not merely anecdotal evidence: scientists from the UK Phenology Network have analysed 25,000 records of trends for more than 700 different species,

With no predictable flowering time for snowdrops now as our seasonal events shift in the calendar, cameraman James Aldred and production runner Louis Rummer-Downing had to be ready to film as soon as they were told the buds had appeared.

recorded by thousands of 'citizen scientists', and found that the majority of these trends indicate that seasonal events are now shifting earlier in spring and later in autumn.

One might of course assume that this is good for nature. After all, surely earlier springs and later autumns give our plants and animals longer to reproduce, and the opportunity to raise more young?

That may indeed be the case in the short term, but in the longer term, if this trend continues, there is the very real danger that nature will go 'out of synch', with devastating consequences for our wildlife. For example, although blue and great tits have shifted their breeding season two or three weeks earlier, to coincide with the earlier emergence of moth caterpillars which they need to feed their hungry broods of young, not all species are able to respond in this way.

Pied flycatchers, which exploit the same food source, are long-distance migrants, so they are unable to respond as rapidly as the resident tits. When the flycatchers arrive back from Africa in mid-to-late April, in some springs they have already missed the opportunity to breed successfully, as by the time their young are in the nest the caterpillars have all gone.

In the highlands of Scotland, other species face very different problems. Ptarmigans and mountain hares depend on snow cover to avoid predators such as golden eagles; and also need low temperatures to prevent competing species moving into their mountain territory. If the temperatures rise and the snow melts, they simply have nowhere else to go.

The future does look bleak for much of our wildlife. The planet as a whole is warming, and all the evidence points to the fact that this will have major effects on the lifecycles of all our plants and animals, effects whose overall consequences are impossible to predict. These will also cause huge problems for wildlife-programme makers in the future.

On a more philosophical note, we define our four seasons by the combination of particular weather patterns and natural events – so what will happen if these all change? And if our seasons eventually become unrecognisable, can we still call them by their traditional names: spring, summer, autumn and winter?

Perhaps this current TV series, and this book, will turn out to be both a celebration of our four seasons and their incredible natural events, and also an elegy – our last chance to enjoy them before they change forever. The last word goes to series producer James Brickell:

'Our seasons are more than just "the weather"; they are a part of our national character. To be able to document them in this series has been both an opportunity and a privilege. We have told an amazing story: part natural, part human, and both tragic and uplifting. We were making a series about a "typical year", yet we all know that in reality there is no such thing. I think that is why we all love the British seasons so much – you just never quite know what will happen!'

When in their winter plumage, ptarmigan are perfectly camouflaged against the snowy tops of the Cairngorm Mountains – making a cameraman's job even more challenging!

WILDLIFE RESOURCES

20 PLACES TO WATCH WILDLIFE IN THE UK

1 ANGLESEY
A varied island with seabird colonies, choughs, terns and a thriving population of red squirrels in the woodlands.

2 BROWNSEA ISLAND, DORSET
One of only two places in southern Britain where you can still see red squirrels (the other is the Isle of Wight), along with sika deer and woodland birds.

3 CASTLE ESPIE, CO. DOWN
This WWT centre is the winter home of pale-bellied Brent geese, which migrate here all the way from Arctic Canada.

4 DONNA NOOK, LINCS
Here you'll find one of the most easily accessible colonies of grey seals, with hundreds of these animals coming ashore every autumn to breed.

5 DUNGENESS, KENT
This shingle promontory juts out into the English Channel, and sees the first landfall for migrant birds, moths and butterflies, especially in spring.

6 EXE ESTUARY, DEVON
Take a cruise up the Exe in winter to see Britain's largest flock of avocets and many other wildfowl and waders.

7 FARNE ISLANDS, NORTHUMBERLAND
These tiny islands off the Northumberland coast are packed with thousands of seabirds in spring and summer, and are home to a colony of grey seals which breed in the autumn.

8 ISLE OF MULL, INNER HEBRIDES
One of Scotland's most accessible and wildlife-packed islands, with white-tailed and golden eagles, otters, seals and seabirds.

9 ISLES OF SCILLY
Britain's most southerly archipelago is a magnet for migrating birds and those who watch them, especially in September and October, when rare wanderers arrive from North America and Siberia.

10 LONDON WETLAND CENTRE
This pioneering urban nature reserve by the Thames is a wildlife gem: birds, bats and butterflies; slow worms and grass snakes; and lots of things for families to do.

11 MARTIN MERE, LANCASHIRE
Another Wildfowl and Wetlands Trust centre with thousands of wintering geese and wild swans.

12 MINSMERE, SUFFOLK
The RSPB's flagship reserve on the coast of Suffolk: home to avocets, marsh harriers and bitterns.

13 NEW FOREST, HAMPSHIRE
Part-wood, part-heath and a haven for wildlife, this is home to a greater variety of insects than anywhere in Britain.

14 NORTH NORFOLK COAST
One of the best places to watch wildlife in Britain, from Snettisham and Titchwell in the west through the seal colony of Blakeney and Cley in the centre, to the Broads in the east.

15 NORTH AND SOUTH UIST, WESTERN ISLES
The fertile islands of the Outer Hebrides are home to breeding waders and the best wild flower displays in Britain, on the rich soils of the machair from May through to July.

16 SHETLAND
Our most northerly outpost is home to vast seabird colonies, with great and Arctic skuas, gannets, puffins and kittiwakes, from March through to July.

17 SOMERSET LEVELS
Former peat diggings have been turned into a fabulous wetland, with otters, bitterns, egrets and cranes, and in winter the biggest starling roost in Britain.

18 SPEYSIDE AND CAIRNGORM, HIGHLANDS
Our last true wilderness, with ptarmigan and mountain hares on the high tops, ospreys and crossbills in the valleys, and red deer roaming the hills.

19 THURSLEY COMMON, SURREY
Britain's premier site for dragonflies with more than 20 different species; plus adders and heathland birds such as woodlark, tree pipit and Dartford warbler.

20 YNYS-HIR, CEREDIGION
A magical woodland reserve in the heart of Wales, with breeding red kites, pied flycatchers and a host of woodland wildlife and wild flowers.

40 THINGS TO SEE

ADDERS

The best opportunity to see adders comes on a bright, clear morning in March or April, when they begin to emerge from their winter quarters. They are sluggish at this time of year, so watch out for them as they bask in the sun to warm up. The New Forest and the Dorset heaths are major adder strongholds, but these snakes can be found in any area of heathland or woodland edge.

AUTUMN MIGRANT BIRDS

Every autumn, millions of birds pass through Britain on their way from their breeding grounds here and in northern Europe to their winter-quarters in southern Europe and Africa. Autumn migration begins as early as July as the first Arctic waders head south and reaches its peak in September and early October when many songbirds pass through, especially at east coast headlands such as Blakeney Point in Norfolk and Spurn Head in Yorkshire.

BADGERS

A controversial animal, especially in dairy farming areas of the south and west, badgers are fascinating but very shy. Your best chance of seeing them is to join an organised visit to a sett in spring or summer, when guides will be able to show you badgers without disturbing them.

BATS

Bats are all around us, yet often all we see of them is a shadowy glimpse in the dark. But go on a bat walk with an expert guide and you will get much closer to these mysterious creatures, as they will be armed with an electronic bat detector which makes their echolocating calls audible to the human ear.

BIRDS OF PREY

Raptors such as the peregrine, merlin, hobby, marsh and hen harrier have all enjoyed a boom in numbers in recent years, and can be seen in a range of habitats from estuaries in winter to moorlands in summer, or even city centres – as peregrines can now be found nesting on tall buildings in many urban areas across Britain.

BLUEBELLS

Britain's favourite flower appears in our woodlands from April into May, creating a carpet of delicate bluish-mauve blooms. Bluebells can be found in ancient woodlands throughout Britain, from the far southwest up into Scotland, where they usually come into flower a few weeks later than in the south.

BUMBLEBEES

One of our most useful insects, pollinating wild and cultivated flowers and crops to help them reproduce, bumblebees are in sharp decline due to the use of pesticides and loss of their habitat. But sunny spring and summer days provide an opportunity to take a closer look, and with practice you could identify some of the 20 or so different species found throughout Britain.

CARNIVOROUS PLANTS

Bizarre as it may seem, some plants eat meat: luring insects such as flies to land on them, and then trapping them so that they can suck out the nutrients! The best known of these is the sundew, which can be seen on boggy heaths in southern Britain and along the west coast to Scotland during the summer months.

CHALKLAND BUTTERFLIES

June and July see the peak emergence of some of our most delicate and beautiful butterflies: those species that specialise on chalk and limestone grasslands, mainly in southern Britain. Species include the dazzling Adonis blue, the more delicate chalkhill blue, and the tiny but exquisite brown Argus.

CUCKOOS

Once a familiar sound of spring across the whole of Britain, cuckoo numbers have declined dramatically in recent years, and now these birds may only rarely be heard in parts of the rural south where they were once common. But they are still thriving in Scotland, and can be heard from mid-April through to late May, uttering their famous call.

DAWN CHORUS

Town and city parks are great places to learn about birdsong: here the birds are usually fairly tame and used to people, so you can confirm the singer's identity by seeing it after you have heard it. It is best to go soon after dawn, before the bulk of visitors arrive, as you will then have the place to yourself. If you want the full dawn chorus experience, though, it's hard to beat an ancient woodland in May.

DEER RUT

Red and fallow deer both take part in an annual 'rut' from late September through to November: when the males gather in combat to win the right to mate with the females. The best places to see the deer rut are the New Forest, parks such as Fountains Abbey in Yorkshire or London's Richmond Park, and on remote Scottish islands such as Rum.

DRAGONFLIES AND DAMSELFLIES

Amongst our most impressive and fascinating insects, these appear on sunny days from April onwards, reaching their peak in numbers in July and August, with a few hardy individuals still on the wing in November. Watch as they patrol a length of waterway before twisting in mid-air to grab a passing insect; or see them close-up as they perch on waterside foliage. Dragonfly hotspots include Wicken Fen in Cambridgeshire, Thursley Common in Surrey and the New Forest.

FUNGI

In autumn, go on a 'fungal foray' with an expert to learn more about these fascinating organisms – neither plant nor animal, but in a kingdom of their own. Mushrooms and toadstools are simply the most visible part of fungi; their unseen parts may stretch underground for huge distances. Fungi make a vital contribution to the ecology of woodlands by breaking down dead vegetable matter. Any wood or shady edge of a field from September to November should provide plenty of opportunities to discover a wealth of different fungi.

GEESE

Hundreds of thousands of wild geese come to Britain every autumn from their northern breeding grounds in Canada, Greenland, Spitsbergen and Siberia, to take advantage of our milder winters and plentiful food. Hotspots include Islay in the Inner Hebrides, the Loch of Strathbeg in eastern Scotland and North Norfolk, home to over 100,000 pink-footed geese from October through to March.

HARES

Hares are mainly nocturnal, so your best chance of seeing them is at dawn or dusk, when they gather in small groups around the edges of fields of grass or arable crops. Most strongholds nowadays are in the east, especially in central Norfolk, Hertfordshire and Cambridgeshire, though they can also be seen elsewhere in rural Britain. Early spring sees male and female hares 'boxing' as they pair up.

KINGFISHERS

Not a rare bird, but they are thinly spread around our rivers and wetlands, so they are never easy to see. Listen out for their high-pitched, repetitive call and watch for a flash of orange and blue as the bird whizzes by! In winter check out coastal estuaries and harbours, as kingfishers will sometimes flee to the coast in hard weather.

LIZARDS

Britain has three native species of lizard: the common and sand lizards, and the very different slow worm, a legless lizard that superficially resembles a small snake. Lowland heaths on warm days from April to September are the best places to see lizards, but slow worms are also frequently found in domestic gardens, especially where there are undisturbed logpiles and compost heaps.

MOTHS

Moths are one of our most overlooked groups of wild creatures: they are everywhere, but because many are nocturnal we only encounter them in car headlights as we return home at night. But use a moth trap – or simply a white sheet and bright torch – on a summer's evening, and you will be amazed at the dozens of colourful moths that are lured in for you to see.

MOUNTAIN WILDLIFE

The Cairngorm plateau in the Scottish Highlands is the only true Arctic-Alpine habitat in Britain. At around 1,300 metres above sea level this is a tough place to live at any time of year, but especially so in the depths of winter when winds can reach gale-force speeds and snow can appear at any moment. But the ski lifts at Cairngorm and Glen Shee enable easy access to the peaks and will provide you with a good opportunity of seeing the specialities of the high tops, including mountain hare, ptarmigan, snow bunting and golden eagle.

NIGHTINGALES

Our most famous songster is also one of the hardest birds to see – skulking in scrubby woodland and singing its heart out, not just at night but sometimes during the day as well. Late April is the best time to see nightingales, just after they have returned from Africa; the male continues to sing during much of May but falls silent and heads back south soon afterwards.

ORCHIDS

Our most spectacular and fascinating flowers are not as rare as you might think: orchids are adaptable plants, so as well as being found on chalk downlands, they also flourish on roadside verges, old industrial sites and even city parks. Nature reserves often hold open days in May, June and July to show off their orchid displays.

OSPREYS

The RSPB reserve at Loch Garten on Speyside in the highlands of Scotland is home to the most visited birds in the country: from April through to August a pair of ospreys breeds here, watched by thousands of visitors each year. Ospreys are a huge success story and can now be seen throughout much of Scotland, with a few pairs in Wales and also at Rutland Water in the heart of England.

OTTERS

Once driven to the edge of extinction in Britain, clinging on only in remote parts of the north and west, otters have made an extraordinary come-back and can now be found on rivers and wetlands throughout the country. Being nocturnal and shy they are not easy to see, but patient waiting alongside a suitable river, especially at dawn or dusk, should eventually yield results.

OWLS

Marshy areas with well-managed grassland are good places to look for hunting short-eared and barn owls, with the peak activity occurring at dawn and dusk. Top sites include the RSPB reserves at Rainham Marshes in East London and Pulborough Brooks in West Sussex. Tawny owls are more often heard than seen, especially in late autumn when they re-establish their territories and so hoot more often.

RED SQUIRRELS

Our only native squirrel has had a tough time in the past century or so; driven back by the more aggressive non-native greys, which also carry a disease that kills the smaller reds. But they are still thriving in Cumbria, the Scottish Highlands and on islands where the greys have not managed to reach: the Isle of Wight and Brownsea Island in Poole Harbour. Autumn is the best time to watch these endearing mammals, as they are active gathering nuts to see them through the winter ahead.

ROCK POOLS

Summer by the seaside provides the ideal opportunity for exploring rock pools at low tide. With patience you can discover fish such as gobies and blennies, shrimps and sea anemones, and a wealth of crustaceans and seaweed. Fascinating.

SEABIRD COLONIES

Britain's seabird colonies are one of our greatest wildlife spectacles: thousands of birds gathering on offshore islands to breed. The largest and most spectacular colonies are off the coasts of west Wales, Scotland and northern England; and the best time to visit is from May through to July, when you can often get very close to iconic species such as puffins, fulmars and Arctic terns.

SEA EAGLES

The sea eagle – also known as the white-tailed eagle – is Britain's biggest and most magnificent bird of prey. Unlike its more elusive cousin, the golden eagle, it is also fairly easy to see, simply by taking a trip to the Isles of Mull or Skye, where it can be watched sitting in its huge nest, or fishing offshore.

SEAL COLONIES

Britain is home to two species of seal: the common or harbour seal, and the larger Atlantic grey seal – almost half the world population of the latter lives here. Seal colonies include the Farne Islands off Northumberland, Donna Nook in Lincolnshire and Blakeney Point in north Norfolk; guided trips are run to all these sites.

SHARKS

Most people would imagine that sharks are creatures of tropical waters and are not found off our coasts. But several species are regular visitors here, notably the giant basking shark – the second largest in the world – that can be found off the west coast of England,

Wales and Scotland from May through to September. As with whales, guided tours by boat are the best way to see this incredible fish.

SONGBIRD FLOCKS

Any ancient woodland during autumn or winter is a good place to catch up with mixed flocks of small songbirds, such as tits, nuthatches, treecreepers and possibly even the rare lesser spotted woodpecker. Good sites include the New Forest and Forest of Dean in the south, Thetford Forest in East Anglia, the oak forests of mid-Wales and, for a different suite of species including siskin, crossbill and crested tit, the Caledonian pine forests of Speyside.

SPRING MIGRANT BIRDS

On fine days in March or April, head to south-coast headlands such as Prawle Point in Devon, Portland Bill in Dorset or Dungeness in Kent: usually the first landing grounds for early migrant birds such as the wheatear, ring ouzel and sand martin.

STAG BEETLES

Our largest, heaviest and most impressive insect, the male stag beetle lives up to his name, bearing huge horns which he uses when in combat with rival males in a miniature version of the deer rut! Stag beetles need a warm climate so are mainly confined to southeast Britain, and can be seen at London parks and commons from late May through to August.

STARLING ROOSTS

On winter evenings, millions of starlings gather at famous roost sites across Britain and perform their amazing acrobatic aerial displays until dusk, when they roost in reedbeds or bushes. Many have disappeared as numbers of this familiar bird have declined, but they can still be seen at Gretna Green in southwest Scotland, near Slimbridge in Gloucestershire, and most famously on the Somerset Levels.

STOATS AND WEASELS

These two superficially similar animals are never easy to see, despite being found across much of rural Britain. Time spent wandering around suitable habitats – traditional farming areas are best – and a lot of patience should eventually bring reward, though. Check out the stoat's larger size and black-tipped tail.

WADER ROOSTS

Tidal estuaries such as the Wash, the Severn and smaller south coast locations like the Exe, Tamar and Chichester and Pagham Harbours support large numbers of waders in autumn and winter. Species include dunlin, knot, redshank, curlew and oystercatcher, with smaller numbers of black-tailed and bar-tailed godwits, grey plover and greenshanks. Avocets – our most elegant wader – can be seen on the Tamar and the Exe.

WATER VOLES

Britain's fastest declining mammal has vanished from many of its former haunts, however water voles can still be seen on some wetlands throughout Britain. Look out for classic signs such as neatly cut grass stems, and small holes in the banks of rivers and streams where the animals nest.

WHALES, DOLPHINS AND PORPOISES

During the spring and summer months our seas are home to a surprising variety of cetaceans – whales, dolphins and porpoises – which come north to feed at this time of year. The best way to see these is to take a specialist boat trip – hotspots include Cornwall, west Wales and the west coast of Scotland.

WINTER WILDFOWL

To see huge flocks of ducks, geese and swans – many of which have flown here all the way from Arctic Siberia, Spitsbergen, Iceland, Greenland and Canada – head for one of the UK's nine Wildfowl and Wetlands Trust Centres any time between October and March. These include the London Wetland Centre, Castle Espie in Northern Ireland, Caerlaverock on the Solway Firth in Scotland, and the Trust's famous headquarters at Slimbridge in Gloucestershire.

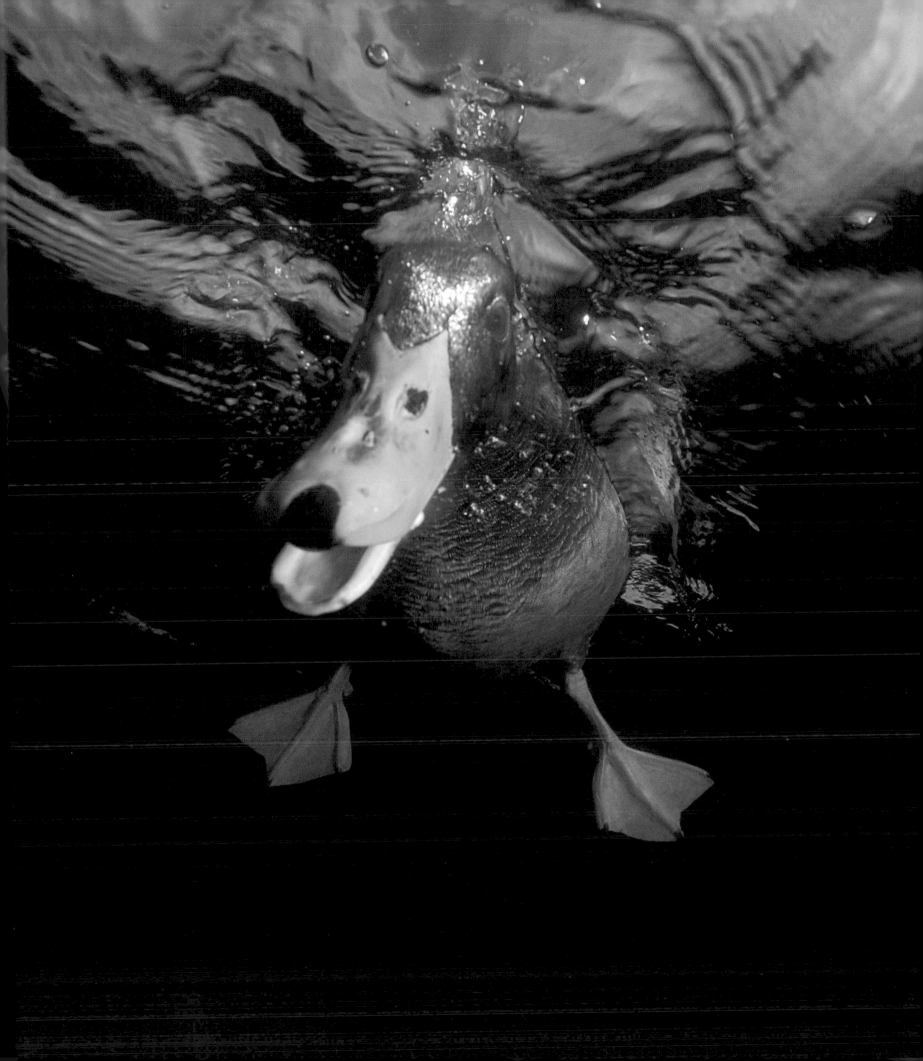

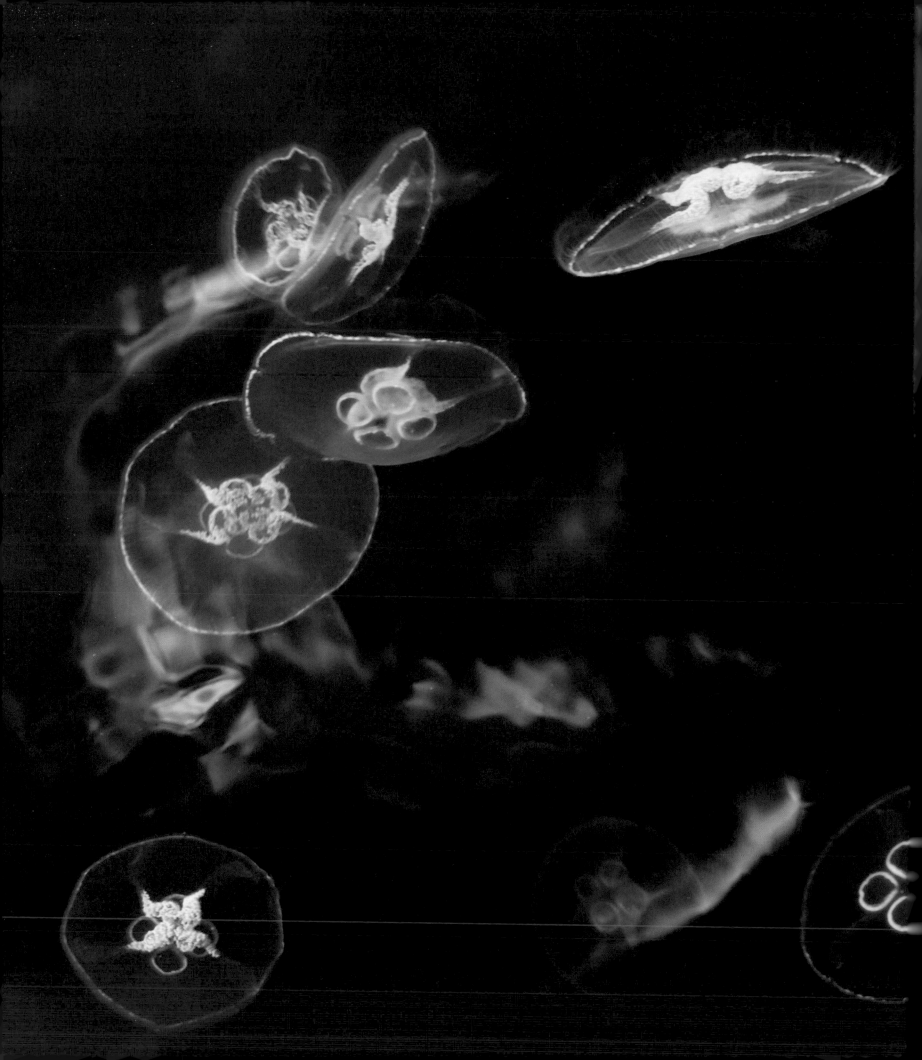

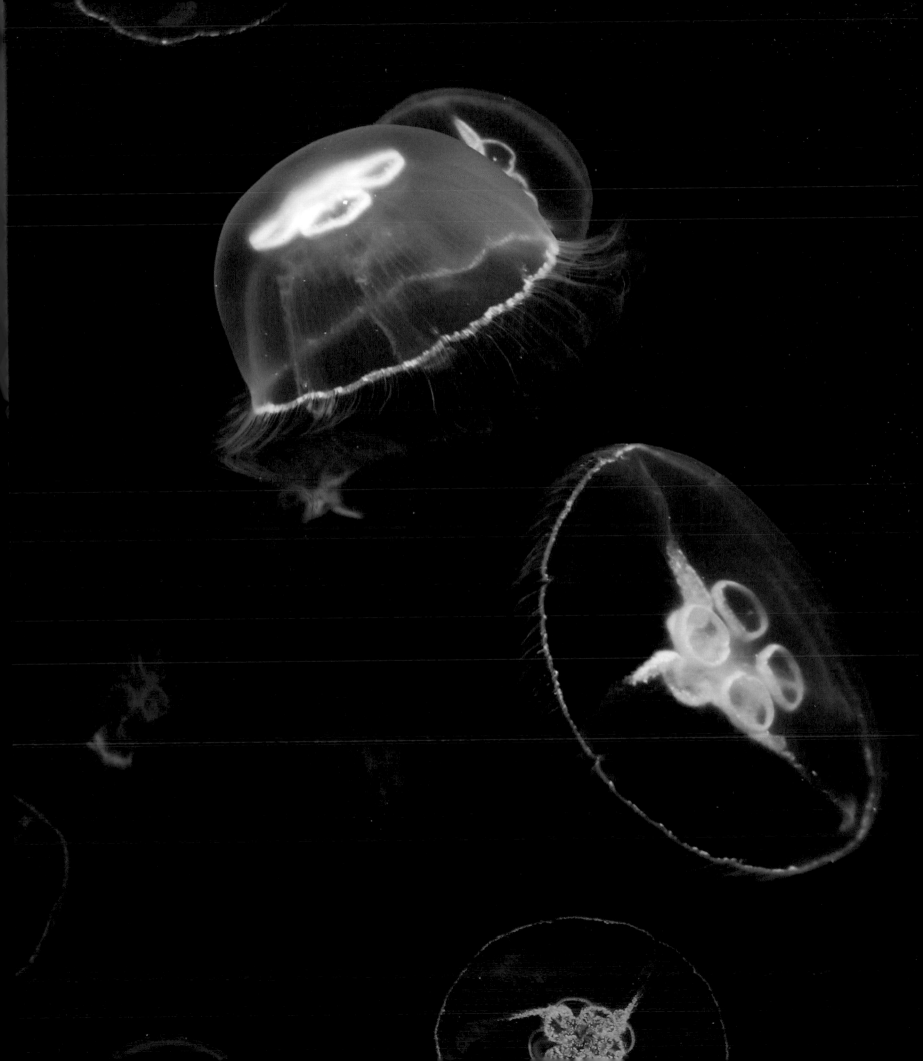

Index

Page numbers in **bold**
indicate an illustration.

CREDITS

The author would like to thank everyone on the TV production team and at Quercus Books for their help and hard work in taking *The Great British Year* from the screen to the page.

Quercus Editions Ltd
55 Baker Street
7th Floor, South Block
London
W1U 8EW

First published in 2013

A catalogue record of this book is available from the British Library.

ISBN 978 1 78087 710 5

Publishing Director: Jenny Heller
Editorial: Ione Walder, Helena Caldon & Ben Brock
Design and picture research: Smith & Gilmour Ltd

Printed and bound in Germany

10 9 8 7 6 5 4 3 2